The Primary Behaviour Cookbook

Developed in conjunction with practitioners and teachers, *The Primary Behaviour Cookbook* provides highly effective, practical strategies for responding to and resolving behavioural issues in primary classrooms.

Consisting of over forty 'recipes', the book's unique format enables practitioners to quickly and easily access information and advice on dealing with specific behaviours. Each 'recipe' details strategies and interventions for immediate application in the classroom setting, considers possible causes of the given behaviour and offers helpful approaches for responding to the child's needs in the longer term. From disengagement to impulsivity, attention-seeking, defiance, bullying, anxiety and aggression, the book's five sections cover a broad spectrum of behaviours falling within five broader categories:

- Getting things done: supporting positive student engagement and achievement
- Dealing with disruption: increasing motivation and skills to facilitate learning
- Social interactions: resolving problematic situations that occur between pupils
- Emotional distress: understanding distress and developing coping strategies
- Behaviours of special concern: recognizing behaviours associated with autism, trauma or abuse.

Underpinned by positive psychology, and emphasizing the importance of constructive relationships, communication, inclusion and child wellbeing, this is an indispensable resource for primary school teachers and assistants, behaviour support consultants, SENDCOs and educational psychologists.

Sue Roffey has been a teacher, educational psychologist and an academic. She is now an Honorary Associate Professor at Exeter University, UK, and Adjunct Associate Professor at Western Sydney University, Australia. She is also Director of Growing Great Schools Worldwide.

'This is an immediately accessible book for busy primary school teachers, covering a wide range of behaviour and welfare issues that teachers face daily. The advice and strategies, are realistically enabling and are based in sound psychology as well as teachers' real experiences. This is a book that enables solution-based approaches to behaviour concerns and challenges, at every level in a school. I commend this book to our busy colleagues in our profession to support respectful, humane and positive behaviour in schools.'

Bill Rogers, Fellow, Australian College of Education; Honorary Life Fellow: Trinity Leeds University and Honorary Fellow at the Graduate School of Education, Melbourne University.

'Wow! This must read book gives practical solutions for common behaviour challenges that are faced by teachers. It is the ideal resource that teachers are looking for! Full of very workable ideas to support teachers, as they nurture good relationships and ensure a climate for learning that unleashes each pupil's potential.'

Neil Hawkes, founder of Values-based Education (VbE) and former primary school headteacher, UK.

The Primary Behaviour Cookbook

Strategies at Your Fingertips

Sue Roffey

Routledge
Taylor & Francis Group

LONDON AND NEW YORK

First published 2019
by Routledge
2 Park Square, Milton Park, Abingdon, Oxon OX14 4RN

and by Routledge
711 Third Avenue, New York, NY 10017

Routledge is an imprint of the Taylor & Francis Group, an informa business

British Library Cataloguing-in-Publication Data
A catalogue record for this book is available from the British Library

Library of Congress Cataloging-in-Publication Data
A catalog record for this book has been requested

ISBN: 978-0-8153-9337-5 (hbk)
ISBN: 978-0-8153-9338-2 (pbk)
ISBN: 978-1-351-18863-0 (ebk)

Typeset in Palatino
by Apex CoVantage, LLC
Printed by CPI Group (UK) Ltd, Croydon CR0 4YY

Contents

Acknowledgements

Thanks to all the educators I have worked with over many years. This includes those who contributed to the first edition, especially my co-author Terry O'Reirdan, together with teachers over the years who have attended courses, tried out and provided feedback on strategies and suggested ideas of their own. Above all, they confirmed repeatedly that what makes the most difference for students – and for teachers – is the quality of relationships across the school and the belief that everyone has strengths and potential.

The 'recipes' here are based in educational and psychological evidence and I would like to acknowledge all those who do this research so we can learn and share good practice.

I am grateful to friends and colleagues across the world, too numerous to mention, who share my commitment to the 'whole child' and their wellbeing. You all help maintain my determination to keep going when sometimes it seems an uphill struggle against a test-driven culture in education that marginalizes our most vulnerable young people.

Debra Magi is due a special mention for giving detailed, helpful feedback on the draft.

Elizabeth Stanley is our extraordinary illustrator. I cannot thank her enough, not only for her wonderful drawings but also her warm and efficient collaboration.

I could not do a fraction of the work I do without the unfailing emotional and practical support of my husband, David, who not only makes tea but checks the finished manuscript, does the formatting and questions unforced errors.

Finally, my thanks to all the children and young people from whom I have learnt so much. This book is dedicated to you and your futures.

Introduction

Several years ago, I was involved in a collaboration with educators exploring issues of concern in the classroom together with strategies they had found useful. This was initially published as an in-house resource and later by David Fulton as *Plans for Better Behaviour in the Primary School*, with Terry O'Reirdan as co-author.

Although this book is based on the original framework and some of the text, the world has moved on a good deal since then. We know more about risk and protective factors for children and what enhances resilience and wellbeing. Many studies have shown that the quality of relationships in the classroom has a major influence on learning, resilience and behaviour. We know that teachers being in charge of proceedings in their class is important but very different from trying to control children – which is exhausting, promotes negative emotions and is usually ineffective. The burgeoning knowledge in positive psychology and neuroscience provides valuable insights and offers many ideas for intervention.

On the other hand, we have alarming increases in the numbers of young people said to be highly anxious or depressed. Others, although not diagnosed with mental illness as such, are simply not doing so well. Many things contribute to the negative emotions that underpin challenging behaviours, but this awareness does not always help in the everyday busyness of the classroom. Teachers themselves have been put under pressure to meet targets, and in many schools this has led to an increased focus on curriculum delivery rather than creativity, compassion, flexibility or fun in the classroom. Children experiencing adversity who present with challenging behaviour may quickly find themselves excluded from the mainstream. As a sense of belonging is important for healthy human development this simply builds up problems for the future.

There are signs the tide is turning, with increasing recognition that wellbeing needs to be placed at the heart of education. Whereas welfare is reactive and the province of senior staff and specialists, everyone in a school is engaged in wellbeing. It is a proactive, universal approach to promote all the protective factors in resilience. This supports pupil engagement and therefore academic outcomes, pro-social behaviour, mental health, resilience and teacher retention. Wellbeing is not a panacea but a framework that fosters optimal outcomes for everyone and a supportive environment when challenges occur.

Two metaphors come to mind when thinking about creating something good and healthy. One is in the garden – sowing a seed in rich soil, watering and feeding regularly, re-planting out at the right time, giving support where needed and watching the plant blossom. The other metaphor is in the kitchen – putting the right ingredients together, mixing them well and baking them at the right temperature for the right amount of time, resulting in something wholesome and nutritious.

Whether it's flowers or cakes, nothing will come out right if you don't pay attention to the environment – the quality of the soil matters, the warmth of the oven is critical. The same is true of behaviour, so this 'cook book' starts with a focus on the emotional climate of the classroom – the oven!

The oven

The emotional climate of the classroom

If your oven is too cold or too hot, nothing you put in to cook will come out right. Similarly, whatever strategies are put into place for behavioural issues, the chance of their effectiveness will be determined by the context – the emotional climate of the classroom.

There is a raft of evidence that supports the importance of the emotional climate of the classroom for both learning and behaviour. How people *feel* in a learning environment matters. This is determined by relationships between peers and between the teacher and the pupil; clear, high expectations and support given to meet these; how people talk to and about each other; a sense of belonging; and the level of good humour in everyday interactions. Much behaviour is an outcome or expression of emotions, so it makes sense at every level to promote the positive. The following is a brief summary of what this entails.

Pupil–teacher relationships

A caring, consistent relationship with a teacher can help a pupil who is struggling feel valued, validated, heard and motivated. The research indicates that a high-quality teacher–child relationship not only reduces the chance of a pupil acting out in the classroom but is also protective in helping to prevent long-term problems that impact on mental health. Having someone believe in the best of you is a powerful protective factor in resilience. This is encompassed in strengths-based approaches, where the pupil is positioned as someone with resources rather than deficits. Ways to establish and maintain positive relationships can be found later in this chapter.

High expectations and clear communications

A class that is chaotic may not be emotionally safe. Children like predictability, and function better when they know exactly what is required of them. Optimal communications are clear, calm and concise and visually supported where possible. Too much information at once can lead to confusion, with pupils getting into trouble for not remembering everything. Routines need to be practiced and positively reinforced. When a student appears unable to do something, check that they have understood, and then ask what they need to do first. High expectations need to apply to all students – no-one is written off as 'unteachable' or a lost cause.

A sense of belonging

Feeling that you belong, that you matter and that you can participate is a fundamental need in psychological development. Our most vulnerable young people are often those who are most quickly marginalized and excluded. Helping them to feel that they have a role in the class, that it matters if they are there and acknowledging their contributions will help prevent them seeking a sense of belonging elsewhere where the outcomes may not be so beneficial.

Strengths-based language

How we speak to and about students (and their families) impacts on self-concept, the expectations of others and the possibility of change.

If you seek and acknowledge the positive qualities that a child possesses, this will do the following: give them something to live up to; increase the chances of this strength being demonstrated; promote a healthy relationship; and re-position the pupil in the eyes of peers.

Alternatively, telling a child that they are lazy, naughty or hopeless will embed a negative self-concept, determine a future negative trajectory and undermine healthy relationships.

Positivity

Positive emotions encourage creativity and problem-solving, whereas negative emotions inhibit clear thinking. It makes sense to actively promote positive emotions in the classroom, so all pupils feel valued, successful, trusted, connected, cared for and liked. Two other emotions also enhance positivity. One is where the teacher models calm, speaking quietly, gaining attention by visual means rather than shouting, and the other is humour. Students value a light-hearted approach where they can occasionally have a laugh together.

Peer relationships

When children think of school they are just as likely to focus on how they get on with their friends as what they are learning. Leaving the social aspects of the classroom to chance may not be the best option. Circle Solutions is a way of encouraging pupils to take responsibility for the emotional climate of the classroom, break down cliques, inhibit bullying and promote friendliness and mutual support.

CIRCLE SOLUTIONS AND THE ASPIRE PRINCIPLES

Many of the activities suggested in the text are based in the Circle Solutions pedagogy for social and emotional learning (SEL). This is intended to not only enhance different understandings and skills but also give students responsibility. When pupils are withdrawn for 'social skills training' they may learn new ways of being, but these are not sustainable. Peers reinforce earlier behaviours because perceptions have not changed. It is therefore essential that SEL takes place as a universal intervention on a regular basis. In Circle Solutions all students and adults take part in activities together. Everything is based in the ASPIRE principles: Agency, Safety, Positivity, Inclusion, Respect and Equity. These are given here individually but in practice they all interact with each other.

Agency

Pupils are not told what to think, but presented with activities that encourage interaction, discussion and reflection on issues. When you give pupils agency, you also hand them responsibility. One example of this is for students to determine the class guidelines at the beginning of the year.

Safety

Circles are a place to think about issues, never incidents. Activities are in pairs, groups or the whole Circle. There is extensive use of the third person (e.g. *'it would make someone angry if . . .'*) so there is no expectation of personal disclosure. No one need say anything if they choose not to.

Positivity

The discussions are primarily solution focused – not what we want to get rid of, but what we want to happen. So instead of talking about bullying, students discuss friendship, inclusion and how we all want to feel in this class. Laughter and playfulness are also part of Circles, as this raises oxytocin levels, which promote connection and resilience.

Inclusion

Everyone is welcomed into the Circle, and pupils are regularly mixed up so they do not stay with their own friendship group. This breaks down barriers. There are clear guidelines on how to respond to uncooperative pupils in order to give them choices and chances to stay within the Circle.

Respect

This is encapsulated in fairness, kindness and consideration. One person speaks at a time and everyone listens. Time is shared fairly. 'Put-downs' in the form of unkind or judgmental comments are not acceptable.

Equity

Everyone has a voice and a turn in any feedback. The teacher is a facilitator of Circles but also a participant. He or she takes part in all activities. This enhances understanding and often relationships. There are flexible arrangements to ensure everyone can join in.

THE TEAM

Family

We need parents/carers as experts on the child, but if we don't relate to them well in the first place, we may get havoc rather than harmony. How you begin communications sets up expectations. Invite parents as experts on their child and ask their advice. Begin any gathering by saying something positive about the student – it will engage parents' attention and help to reduce their anxiety/embarrassment/anger. You may want to sensitively ask questions about what happens at home and if they share your concerns. Keep initial interactions informal, low-key and positive. Many parents are anxious about their child's wellbeing and may feel blamed for any behavioural difficulties. Showing that you have the child's best interests at heart and that you are looking to work constructively with families means taking their context and concerns into account. Sometimes it may not be parents who have the best relationship with the child – it might be helpful to have a grandparent or aunt come along. If a meeting involves other professionals make sure that you ask a parent to bring someone along with them. This provides balance, emotional support, someone to talk to afterwards and someone to take care of any little ones. If you find yourself faced with an abusive family member stay in a public place and send for assistance. Do not attempt to argue but let them run out of steam. Then, if you can, arrange to see them when things have calmed down. De-brief with a trusted colleague.

Teachers

Teachers need to focus on what they have control or influence over - such as expectations, relationships and conversations, and *not* spend precious time or energy on things they cannot change – such as pupil prior experience, family or current educational policy. Teacher wellbeing is critical – stressed, under-valued and under-resourced individuals in the classroom are less likely to have what it takes to turn behaviour around, though many are working miracles without recognition.

School leaders

The values, vision and communication skills of school leaders are central to developing a school that embraces all children as worthwhile and puts well-being at the heart of its endeavours. The outcome is not only an increase in positive behaviour but also academic engagement and outcomes. A wise school leader will also find ways to acknowledge and value staff.

Other professionals

Sometimes more expertise is needed in a school – especially for those pupils who have experienced trauma, abuse or who are on the autistic spectrum. Educational psychologists are the lynchpin between health and education. Most will have been trained to work systemically across the school, not just to provide assessment or counselling for individuals. Make friends with your local service and see what they have to offer. This is likely to include consultation and training. Ask your EP how best to work with challenging parents, for instance, or to provide a workshop on sleep. They do not have all the answers but will be able to make suggestions you may not have thought about. There are also specific organizations, such as the National Autistic Society, that have a wealth of useful information on their websites. Many such organizations are listed in **Resources and further reading** at the end of this book.

ALTERNATIVES TO A BEHAVIOURIST MODEL

A behaviourist model asserts that extrinsic rewards will increase wanted behaviours and punishment will reduce negative behaviours. This is the basis of many school behaviour policies and reflects western culture. Such policies may work with children who are mostly doing well but temporarily go off the rails: just expressing disappointment may be enough to persuade them to change their behaviour. Pupils experiencing tough situations and high levels of negative emotion are, however, less likely to care about getting into trouble for breaking the rules. We need to think differently and relationally about these young people and give them agency, connection and encouragement to try out different ways of being and becoming.

Intrinsic rewards

Replace extrinsic rewards such as stickers with intrinsic ones where possible. Intrinsic rewards are linked to mastery, autonomy and purpose: this could include having a sense of achievement, rising to a challenge, participation, creating something worthwhile, incrementally getting better at something and feeling efforts are valued. Raising awareness of positive feelings could also include commentary on a student's increased understanding and learning, strengths development and noting who will be proud of what they have done. Stickers and certificates that acknowledge a student's efforts may be useful in communicating progress for both parents and pupils but the intrinsic reward of having this noticed by people who matter is what is really important. You do not want improved behaviour to depend on stickers but on the choices a student makes for themselves.

Sanctions and consequences

Similarly, punishment that has little connection with a pupil's behaviour can be meaningless, ineffective and potentially stir resentment – this includes detentions or going on report. On the other hand, natural consequences, respectfully delivered, can be useful. Examples could be: efforts to repair what is damaged or tidy what has been messed up; a limited time without access to equipment that has been used inappropriately; helping out with something following uncooperative behaviour; identifying strengths for someone to whom the student has been unkind; students in conflict left together to come up with their own solution (the whole class may need some training in how to do this); or time-out to regain self-control or for reflection on an event.

Praise and feedback

Bland praise (*'well done'*, *'good for you!'*) can easily be dismissed by a student who finds it difficult to think positively about themselves. Feedback needs to be specific and relate to effort rather than ability, e.g. *'Well done on that maths assignment, you worked really hard and deserve your good mark'*. Carol Dweck's mindset theory shows that praising *ability* leads to a fixed mindset – you either have the skill or not – whereas praising *effort* leads to a growth mindset – the harder you try the better you will get. This can apply to behaviour as well as academic learning. Second hand or indirect praise has particular benefits in building positive relationships – this is where a pupil finds that you have said something positive about them to another person.

A note about labelling

There is much debate about the validity and use of some psychiatric labels. Although the term 'disorders' can be appropriate in some instances, such as autistic spectrum disorder (ASD), they imply that the 'problem' exists solely within the individual rather than in their reaction to adverse circumstances. This is why the focus here is on an interactive rather than medical 'within-child' model of behaviour, looking at what is possible to change within context, utilizing strengths-based rather than deficit language.

The alternative to medical diagnosis is known as 'formulation', a process which takes into account both the individual's history and the contexts in which difficulties appear.

It takes time!

If you take things out of the oven too soon, they will not be cooked! Just the same, there are no quick fixes for children whose behaviour may be the outcome of adversity and/or negative learning; BUT small, consistent, positive interactions lead to big changes over time.

Ingredients

ESSENTIAL MAIN INGREDIENT: POSITIVE TEACHER–PUPIL RELATIONSHIPS

This section gives ideas on how to relate most effectively with all students and in particular those whose behaviour might undermine a teacher's sense of competence and confidence.

Do

Smile! It conveys warmth and liking.

Where possible, be in the classroom before pupils arrive and welcome everyone by name.

Use 'I statements' rather than 'you statements' e.g. *'I am finding this noise level too high'*, rather than *'you are being too noisy'*. People find it easier to listen to 'I statements'.

Ask questions where possible. Requiring a response means the student has to pay more attention to what you are saying rather than it going in through one ear and out the other. These questions need to convey curiosity rather than interrogation, e.g. *'I have noticed that . . . and now I wonder . . . what do you think?'*

Find out something about the lives and interests of students, especially those who are more troublesome. It is particularly valuable to explore things you have in common, e.g. supporting the same team, having a pet, liking the same music, watching the same TV program – you might want to make an effort to tune in to what your pupils are watching! This facilitates brief, regular conversations e.g. *'great match, what a score'*; *'how's your new baby doing?'*. These can be momentary, but reap great benefits as they convey interest and liking.

Let students know you believe in the best of them and that they have something to offer.

Comment briefly on the strengths that you have observed and give opportunities to demonstrate these.

Notice and comment on positive behaviours, small changes and effort.

Label *behaviours* as unwanted, but combine this with saying something positive about the pupil – many students assume that a teacher criticizing their behaviour means they don't like or value them, so separate the behaviour from the child.

Structure success experiences, so the child has a sense of achievement, however small.

Acknowledge that the first time you do something it is hard, but it gets easier with practice.

Celebrate diversity in active ways – everyone is unique, but we also have much in common.

Offer choices to increase agency, so pupils begin to make their own decisions and therefore take more responsibility: limited choices are usually easier than open-ended ones.

Keep your voice low – when you want the attention of the class arrange a visual signal with them rather than raising the volume. If you have visually impaired pupils, combine this with a soft musical sound.

Use second-hand praise. Tell someone else about a pupil's progress and ensure it gets back to them or tell someone else in their hearing. This is more powerful than direct praise.

Acknowledge emotions – e.g. *'I can see that you are feeling angry/disappointed/ upset/excited'*. Once this happens the student has less need to express feelings more loudly to be heard.

Demonstrate fairness and consistency – have the same behavioural expectations for everyone.

Be gentle – with pupils and with yourself.

Show that you too make mistakes on occasion – this relieves pupil anxiety about being perfect. It also models persistence and resilience in the face of adversity.

Be willing to apologise when you have not understood, or have jumped to conclusions.

Treat students with respect at all times. This helps maintain your integrity and wellbeing.

Helpful phrases:

You seem to be having some difficulty here. What should you be doing? Tell me.

What would help? How can I help?

What you did manage was fine. What might be the next step?

I like the way you. . .

I can see you are upset – but you must still consider others.

No one is allowed to hurt other children in this class. You must not hurt other people, and no one is allowed to hurt you.

What might you do to make it better? What do you think should happen next?

I'll give you a few minutes to think about this/settle down/calm down.

Tomorrow is another day – let's try again then.

Do not

Single out students in the first instance. When you want to address a behaviour begin by speaking to the whole class, e.g. *'You are all taking a long time to settle down. I see some of you are ready, that's great. Now everyone please.'* If necessary, talk to individuals privately.

Make overt comparisons with other pupils or siblings – this can lead to resentment.

Make value judgments based on family, culture, ethnicity or gender. It should no longer need to be said but is still evident in many institutions.

Take a pupil's behaviour personally. It is unlikely to have anything to do with you even though you appear to be in the firing line.

Go on the defensive. This escalates confrontation and conflict.

SPECIAL INGREDIENTS – STARRED STRATEGIES

These strategies come up often in the Recipes that follow, so they are not spelled out in full each time. Where you see a *, e.g. '*Assertiveness skills', in the text, it refers back to these strategies.

Assertiveness skills

When faced with a potential conflict there are several options: aggression/ducking out/appropriate assertiveness. Children need to know they have choices, and that being assertive is empowering, makes them feel good and does not have negative consequences. In summary, being assertive means stating clearly what you feel and what you want to happen, using an 'I statement', e.g. *'I don't like you calling me names, I want you to stop it.'* Students are encouraged to use these statements and then walk away from the situation, preferably to a supportive adult.

Breathing

Deliberate regular breathing reduces heart-rate and therefore anxiety. All children can easily be taught how to do this. Teachers can model this for students who are angry or otherwise agitated, encouraging them to copy.

Calming corner

This is an area in the classroom to support children to develop self-regulation, i.e. calm themselves down when strong emotions take over and/or provide brief respite from stress. It could contain items such as stress balls, stretchy resistance bands, a pot of bubbles, a soft cushion, noise cancelling headphones, puzzles, focus items such as a snow-globe or kaleidoscope and visual posters to encourage breathing, mindfulness and yoga poses. There need to be clear criteria for entry and to be time-limited.

Catch the child being good

Making a point of verbally noting when a pupil – or pupils – are behaving as required. So often the focus is on what is not going well. This shifts the emphasis of conversation and affirms what is expected.

Circle of friends

This is a structured intervention where a small voluntary group supports an individual student experiencing social difficulties. See **Resources and further reading** for more information about how to set this up.

Circle Solutions (CS) activities

This is a whole class intervention that takes place within a Circle incorporating the ASPIRE principles (see earlier). This creates an opportunity to explicitly teach the behaviours/attitudes/values you want to see in your classroom. Although one pupil might be the main target of this intervention, doing the activity with others will not only enhance individual skills for everyone, it will also reinforce these by having peer support and involvement. Many of the strategies here can be developed within a Circle Solutions session.

Conflict resolution

Help pupils learn how to resolve everyday differences. These steps will help:

1   Take some space to calm down – you cannot resolve an issue at the height of emotion.
2   Both pupils state wants and needs (do not focus on the details of what happened).
3   Both pupils state what their intention was – often they have the same or similar.
4   Define the problem – what is this really about? It is often an issue such as fairness.
5   Pupils work together to find a solution which feels OK for both of them. They might need to think through the pros and cons of various options before choosing one.
6   Check that the solution is safe and fair for all.
7   Commend pupils for their skills.

Cooperative working

Students are given a task and work together to complete this. Each individual has a particular role and responsibility so that success is dependent on the work of everyone in the group. This enhances the skills needed in team-work.

Co-regulation of emotions

Some pupils do not have the skills to self-regulate their emotions, so need adult support to do this. This usually happens with parents in infancy, but a version can take place with teachers in the classroom. Although co-regulation is more often used with children on the autistic spectrum others can also benefit. It is where a trusted adult tunes into the child and shows empathy for what they are feeling by mirroring their facial expressions. They give a name to the feelings and a model for the child to copy in reducing intensity.

Externalizing problems

This strategy is taken from narrative therapy. It refers to the problem as separate from the child and getting in the way of their better selves. It is a light-hearted response that may make the student smile. An example might be; *'that rotten temper has been getting the better of you – today, tell it to give you a rest.'*

Face-saving

Sometimes students back themselves into a corner and need help to get out that will enable them to save face and avoid embarrassment or humiliation. You could do one of the following: give them time to complete an instruction; offer to do something with them; ask them to demonstrate strengths; admit an error yourself; ask them to do something else; ask them to show/support a peer.

Feelings feedback

Asking how a pupil feels about a positive achievement or behaviour will help them tune into what brings them good feelings and what maintains the negative.

Mistakes as part of learning

Everyone makes mistakes and young people need to not fear them. Very few people get things right the first time. All tasks become easier with practice. It will help if mistakes are overtly accepted as part of learning in the classroom and the teacher also acknowledges making them from time to time.

Mnemonics

These are a way of triggering memory, and are popular with children. For example:

> Give me FIVE – Focus, Ignore distractions, Voice off, Eyes down
> or RACK – Random Act of Classroom Kindness.

Students will come up with many more if you give them the chance!

Natural consequences

Although punishment itself rarely changes behaviour, natural consequences related to the misdemeanour make sense to the pupil. When these are respectfully delivered, they both maintain high expectations and are less likely to damage relationships.

Partial agreement

Rather than get into an argument with a pupil, see where you can agree with them. Once you have done this it is easier to ask them to do something differently.

Paula Pane

Have a drawing of a life-sized child on the classroom window or use a puppet or soft toy instead. The idea is to have a conversation with an imaginary person about the class and how well they are doing (or sometimes not doing). This brings in some humour, reinforces expectations, and does not single out individuals. Works brilliantly!

Peer support

This is a voluntary arrangement where volunteer students are trained to be mentors or buddies. Activities can take place in the playground or classroom and include reading or other academic support, conflict mediation or disability support. Peer support may also be less formal where students are asked to be the first port of call for a query from a less confident pupil. This needs to be a shared task and monitored carefully so that it does not put undue pressure on any individual.

Permission

This is sometimes known as paradoxical instruction. The student is given leave to continue with what they are doing until they are ready to choose something different. This undermines defiance and does not give attention to misbehaviour. It can only be used when behaviour is not endangering anyone. An example might be that a pupil has climbed under a desk. Rather than spend time and energy persuading them to come out – and engaging in a game where they hold all the cards – you might say, *'let me know when you want to start on your project again'*. You might want to add; *'I am impressed with what you have done so far'*.

Personal bests

For children who are never going to be academic stars in a competitive environment, it makes more sense for them to compete against themselves. The conversation of personal bests needs to permeate the class, so that all pupils can celebrate achievements for those unlikely to otherwise receive public accolades.

Personal monitoring

This intervention gives the student maximum agency. The pupil is asked what they want to aim for in their class, in terms of improving aspects of their behaviour and learning. They are encouraged to choose actions that have the most chance of being successful. They keep their own record of how well they do and show this to the teacher at the end of the day. If they have their own book with the chosen actions written on each page, they can personalize this, so it becomes something of which to be proud.

Positive reinforcement

The other side of the coin of ignoring unwanted behaviour is to give the oxygen of attention for what is wanted. Smile, give eye contact, praise the specific behaviour, e.g. '*well done for* . . .'. Sometimes this has to be a bit over the top to work! And expect it to take time for pupils who have become used to getting negative attention.

Proximity praise

The teacher chooses students near to the one who is not responding to request and briefly thank them for the specific behaviour required, e.g. '*Thank you Molly for waiting quietly*', '*Well done Pedro for looking this way*'. This alerts the pupil to what is expected and gives attention to those who are compliant.

Restorative conversation

This is based in the restorative justice approach, which seeks ways of addressing conflict and repairing harm. It includes all parties involved and aims for a win-win outcome. It requires training and skilled facilitators to embed restorative approaches effectively across a whole school, but the following is the basic framework for a restorative conversation. It takes place after the incident (but the same day) in a private place. This gives everyone time to calm down and reflect on what happened. Restorative conversations are always voluntary.

- What happened?
- What were you thinking and feeling at the time?
- What do you think and how do you feel now?
- Who has been affected by this?
- What's needed to put things right?
- How can we make sure this doesn't happen again?

Those affected by the actions of the perpetrators are asked to state their reactions, how they felt, what was hard for them and what they would like to happen to make things better.

Safe touch massages

Some children rarely experience positive touch. Possibly the only time they are touched is to be physically hurt. Positive touch is linked to overall wellbeing so this will have greater impact than may at first seem apparent. All children stand in a circle and each turns to their left. They ask the person whose back is in front of them for permission to touch them in this activity: '*May I do this massage on your back?*' If they say no, then hands stay by the child's side. For all others, the teacher reads out the following and the children make the appropriate moves on their partner's back.

Rainstorm:

Clouds are gathering in the sky – (flat hands move across the back)

A few spots of rain fall from the sky – (one finger on each hand gently taps the back)

Then the rain gets heavier and heavier – (all fingers tap across the back)

There is thunder – (the fist gently pummels the back as a cat might do with a blanket)

And lightning – (the side of the hands cross the back diagonally from bottom to top and then top to bottom)

Gradually the rain eases – (back to one finger tapping) – until it stops altogether

Soon the sun comes out – (both flat hands make large circular motions across the back).

Pizza:

First you roll out the dough – (flat hands up and down the back)

Then you spread the tomato mixture across the base – (hands going from side to side)

Next sprinkle on the grated cheese – (fingers flutter across the back)

Think of your favourite ingredients and add these – (fingers circle or tap for pepperoni or pieces of pineapple)

Now it goes into the oven to bake – (hands stay flat on the back)

And when it is ready it comes out and you cut it into 8 pieces – (side of hands across back, up and down, across and diagonally) – Yum!

Star of the day

Each pupil has a turn in being 'special' for a day. The Star has special privileges as well as responsibility for that day. The role is a right, not to be used as a reward or taken away as a sanction. In a Circle Solutions session the Star is asked to leave the room whilst all other pupils make positive comments that are written up by the teacher. The pupil is then asked to return, and they are told – *'this is what this class thinks about you.'* The comments are read out and given to the student. This activity is aimed at changing self-concepts and promoting a strengths perspective.

Strengths-based conversation

This conversation between teacher and pupil reframes behaviour in terms of a student's strengths and then looks to a student's qualities for repair, e.g.

> *'I know you attacked Josh because you are protective about your mum. You are a loyal and caring person. But you hurt Josh. What could you have done instead?'*

'You have a great sense of humour, Emily, but when would be a better time to make everyone laugh?'

Success opportunities

This is a strategy aimed at changing self-concept for children who see themselves negatively. It entails the teacher presenting the pupil with a task (academic or non-academic) where they are guaranteed a successful outcome, however minor. This can be achieved with peer support or independently.

Tactical ignoring

There are different grades of ignoring – the main reason for this is not to reward unwanted behaviour by giving it attention.

- Ignore it altogether, do not give eye-contact or speak.
- Speak quietly and briefly but otherwise not engage.
- Give an instruction and walk away.
- Say briefly in which circumstance you will respond – e.g. *'when the shouting stops I will listen'*. You have to stick with this or it won't work in the longer term.

See 'Positive reinforcement' above.

'Take Two' scripts

You pretend to be a film director. When a pupil says or does something that is inappropriate you say *'Cut!'* then *'Take Two'*, and say the script that you want the student to copy. Even if they do not follow through, it provides the necessary learning about a more acceptable alternative. It also reduces the heat in a stressful situation.

Take-up time

This is beneficial for both the pupil and the teacher. Make a request to the student, check their understanding and then say, *'see how you get on, I'll come back in a few minutes/later'*. Standing over students can be intimidating.

Task analysis

This is breaking down a task into small manageable steps, clarifying the sequence needed and beginning with the first step. This stops a task being overwhelming for a student who is struggling and provides an opportunity for positive feedback.

Task priority

Let the student know what you are seeking from them:

- Content and exploration of ideas;
- Length;
- Accuracy (e.g. spelling, sums);
- Presentation: how neat the work is;
- Problem-solving: evidence of working things out.

Some students struggle with multiple expectations. Evaluate on the basis of your stated priority.

The look!

This is a silent signal to the student that you have noticed what they are doing/ not doing and implies the message to get back on track. You may need to begin by saying their name and/or moving nearer. Making direct eye contact from under your eyebrows and then raising them quizzically is about right!

Ticket out the door

Pupils are asked to write the most interesting thing they learnt that day and give the teacher that 'ticket out the door' as they leave to go home. Alternatives could be something they felt proud of, tried hard with or demonstrated a strength.

Traffic lights

Most pupils have a concept of traffic lights. Students who are struggling to stay calm can be offered this strategy to give them agency in a situation. They have three cards in red, green and orange. The green card uppermost indicates all is going well and they feel calm; the orange card indicates that they are beginning to feel agitated and may need some support; the red card indicates an imminent loss of control. Pupils may be given permission to take themselves out of a situation once the red card is shown – perhaps going outside the classroom to cool down, fetch a glass of water or just breathe. Teachers using this strategy report that it is rarely misused and gives students greater awareness of their feelings and agency to take positive action to reassert self-control.

Visual cues

Some pupils experiencing receptive or expressive language difficulties may present with challenging behaviour. For these students, as well as those learning English, visual cues used in conjunction with words can help.

Content

Using a solution- and strengths-based approach, the aim of this book is to not simply eliminate problems but to focus on desired changes. The approaches suggested are intended to maintain maximum respect for the student – however difficult they may be – be clear about what is and is not acceptable in the classroom and support teacher integrity and wellbeing. It is acknowledged that some pupils will have behaviours that fit into several categories. Each 'recipe' page is divided into the following sections.

- What is the problem – so what are you aiming for? You may not reach your target, but this puts you on the right track towards a desired outcome, and goes beyond simply trying to eliminate difficulties.
- What do you need to know that will help put appropriate strategies into place? This includes identifying what is happening when the child *is* behaving in the desired way. This will focus on how to get more of a wanted behaviour rather than less of an unwanted one. Knowing a bit about what a child is dealing with, what may be reinforcing the behaviour and what has helped in the past also gives guidance as to what might be more effective.
- What might you do today in the classroom when challenging behaviour is occurring? Some of this may depend on what you have already put in place in whole class activities. The efficacy of short term strategies will often depend on the quality of the relationship that has been established with the student.
- What will support longer term change? This includes how we support students to think and feel more positively about themselves and others. It focuses on developing strengths, understanding, skills, resilience and responsibility.

What you do in the classroom today needs to be congruent with plans for longer term change.

The behaviours are divided into five sections. There is frequently overlap between these, and some pupils will be displaying aspects of all five. We begin with those that are often the most annoying and frustrating, through to behaviours that are distressing, confusing and sometimes extreme.

Getting things done

Some children have difficulty settling into the routine of a school day, beginning and/or completing set work and engaging appropriately in classroom activities. This section addresses the many ways this might be exhibited in the classroom, and what teachers might do to support positive student engagement and achievement.

Dealing with disruption

This is where pupils go one step further than not settling and actively disrupt others. They do this in various ways that go from being mildly irritating to being actively defiant. Here we are looking to increase the motivation and skills that enable students to behave in ways that facilitate learning for themselves and others.

Social interactions

Many of the problematic situations that occur are between pupils. Social difficulties require social solutions so many of the longer term change activities here are based in whole class intervention.

Emotional distress

Many challenging behaviours in school are an expression of high levels of emotion and can include anxiety, anger or depression. Here we explore what might be going on for young people and seek ways in which they can develop coping strategies that are less harmful for themselves and others.

Behaviours of special concern

Sometimes a student behaves in a way that is bewildering for teachers and leaves them unsure what to do for the best. Some of these behaviours are indicative of autism, some of trauma and others of abuse. Although specialist advice is valuable for all these situations, this section is designed to help educators have some understanding of how to recognize these behaviours, what responses are appropriate and what might help that young person in the classroom.

These are followed by a section on **Resources and further reading**, including links to further information and ideas.

Bibliography

Brackett, M.A., Reyes, M.R., Rivers, S.E., Elbertson, N.A., & Salovey, P. (2011). Classroom emotional climate, teacher affiliation and student conduct. *Journal of Classroom Interaction, 46*(1), 27–36.

Durlak, J.A., Weissberg, R.P., Dymnicki, A.B., Taylor, R.D., & Schellinger, K.B. (2011). The impact of enhancing students' social and emotional learning: A meta-analysis of school-based universal interventions. *Child Development, 82*(1), 405–432.

Dweck, C.S. (2006). *Mindset: The New Psychology of Success.* New York: Random House.

Fredrickson, B. (2009). *Positivity: Ground-Breaking Research to Release Your Inner Optimist and Thrive.* Oxford: One World Publications.

Hansberry, B. (2016). *A Practical Introduction to Restorative Practice in Schools: Theory, Skills and Guidance.* London: Jessica Kingsley Publishers.

Hromek, R., & Roffey, S. (2009). Games as a pedagogy for social and emotional learning. 'It's fun and we learn things'. *Simulation and Gaming, 40*(5), 626–644.

Johnson, D.T., & Johnson, R.W. (1994). An overview of cooperative learning. In J. Thousand, A. Villa and A. Nevin (Eds.), *Creativity and Collaborative Learning.* Baltimore: Brookes Press.

McCashen, W. (2005). *The Strengths Approach: A Strengths-Based Resource for Sharing Power and Creating Change.* Bendigo: St Luke's Innovative Resources.

Newton, C., & Wilson, D. (2017). *Creating Circles of Friends: A Peer Support and Inclusion Workbook.* Nottingham: Inclusive Solutions.

Noble, T., McGrath, H., Roffey, S., & Rowling, L. (2008). *Scoping Study Into Approaches to Student Wellbeing.* Canberra: Department of Education, Employment and Workplace Relations.

O'Connor, E.E., Dearing, E., & Collins, B.A. (2011). Teacher–child relationship and behaviour problem trajectories in elementary school. *American Educational Research Journal, 48*(1), 120–162.

Pianta, R.C., & Walsh, D.J. (1996). *High Risk Children in Schools: Constructing Sustaining Relationships.* New York: Routledge.

Roffey, S. (2011). *Changing Behaviour in Schools: Promoting Positive Relationships and Wellbeing.* London: Sage Publications.

Roffey, S. (2014). *Circle Solutions for Student Wellbeing.* London: Sage Publications.

Roffey, S. (2017). 'Ordinary magic' needs ordinary magicians: The power and practice of positive relationships for building youth resilience and wellbeing. *Kognition & Paedagogik, 103.*

Roffey, S. (2017). The ASPIRE principles and pedagogy for the implementation of social and emotional learning and the development of whole school wellbeing. *International Journal of Emotional Education, 9*(2), 59–71.

Thorsborne, M., & Blood, P. (2013). *Restorative Practices in Schools.* London: Jessica Kingsley Publishers.

Section 1: getting things done

Section 1: getting things done

Pupils who do not settle to work can take up more teacher time and energy than almost anything else. Their behaviour may include not listening or following instructions, being distracted, avoiding or refusing work, not completing set tasks or simply being helpless.

Although it has become increasingly commonplace for adults to label such pupils as having attention-deficit-hyperactivity disorder (ADHD), it is more helpful to work out what is going on in the child's life in order to ascertain what best to do. Labelling a child in this way gives them the impression that they 'can't help it', and others the idea that they do not have to change their approach, as responsibility for change lies with the student. Psychotropic drugs might provide immediate relief but are rarely a long-term solution

Healthy young children are naturally motivated to learn, although not necessarily in the way formal education demands. Not settling to or finishing directed tasks may be linked to one or more of the following:

- High levels of natural energy/insufficient opportunity for physical play
- An overstimulating environment that inhibits a focus on just one activity
- Poor impulse control
- Low confidence and anxiety about performance – anxiety is now a major mental health concern for children
- Not having learnt to listen/lack of listening practice
- Not having experience of activities that have a beginning, middle and end, e.g. regularly disrupted meals, TV programs, conversations etc.
- Low expectations of independence – others doing things for them
- Mismatch between task and ability – at both ends of the spectrum, too difficult or not challenging enough
- Nothing to link the task to – prior work, interest, something meaningful or enjoyable
- Immaturity or general learning difficulties
- A need for autonomy and choice
- Auditory processing or language difficulties
- Not understanding the purpose of the task
- Stress or trauma leading to inability to focus and possibly hypervigilance
- Being on the autistic spectrum
- Nutritional issues
- Not having enough sleep
- Being unwell or hungry.

If either of the last two are an issue then this needs to be addressed as a priority, both in school and at home. Increasing numbers of children are failing to have their basic needs for nutrition, shelter, warmth or adequate clothing met and some schools are now providing breakfast clubs for pupils. Poverty is stressful for families, and children who come to school with high levels of the stress hormone cortisol will be neither in an optimal physical condition nor in the best frame of mind to learn. If a child falls asleep in a classroom find them somewhere comfortable and contact parents about your concerns. You may find it helpful to ask your educational psychologist to give a talk to parents about the importance of sleep and how to establish a positive sleep routine at home.

Procrastination

For some children – as for many adults – the problem with settling to work is simple procrastination. This is where anything that is fun, easy and immediate takes precedence over the hard, the meaningful and the longer term. Introduce children to the idea of the procrastination monkey, who takes the steering wheel of your brain away from good thinking and suggests you do a hundred and one other things rather than what you had planned to do. Children need to be aware of things that distract them. One answer is to do the first thing you have to do NOW – and then the next – and so on. One useful acronym is BANJO – Bang a Nasty Job Off! Often it takes less time and effort than you imagine and gives you the satisfaction of crossing something off a list. Taking regular breaks is not procrastination, so long as these are planned and the main task is proceeding well!

'Flow'

Csikszentmihalyi (1990) describes the concept of 'flow' as the optimal place of learning. This is where there is a balance between the challenge of the task and the skill of the student. If the task is too easy or too difficult for the level of ability flow cannot occur and boredom, apathy or anxiety results.

Agency

The younger the child the more self-directed they will want to be. Giving some limited choices may help with this. Over time they should be more able to focus on direction. Some parents may need guidance to support this at home, especially praising effort and independence. For older children, autonomy is still a powerful motivator. Although teachers have little freedom with regard to curriculum targets they may have some choice as to how to teach.

Projects, group work, *co-operative learning and focusing on *personal bests are all ways that give children more control of the learning process and are more fun.

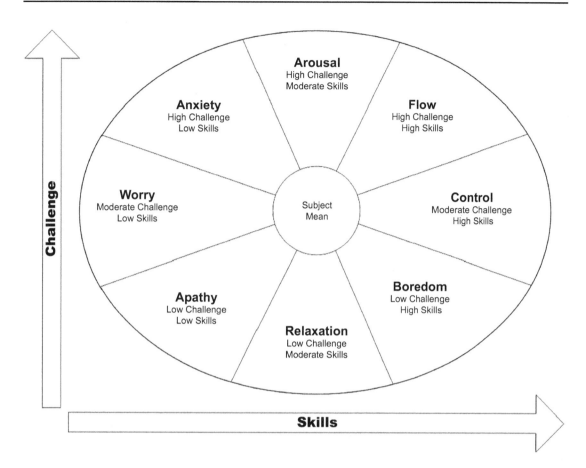

Growth mindset

Many teachers are now aware of the difference between a fixed mindset and a growth mindset. This theory, developed by Carol Dweck (2006), says that children with a fixed mindset believe they either have an ability or not: low marks tell them they don't have this particular ability so no point in trying. A growth mindset is where children believe that it is effort that makes the difference to progress and achievement. How we talk with children when they achieve something fixes one or other of these mindsets. For example:

- *Well done, George, you clever boy.* Fixed mindset.
- *Well done, George, you worked hard on that.* Growth mindset.

Staying active

No child should be sitting in the same place for a long time. Not only it is unnatural for them developmentally, there is also evidence that physical activity stimulates cognitive pathways. Make it routine that everyone stands up and moves their bodies about for a few minutes every half hour or so. An active classroom is more appropriate for young children than a silent, stationary one.

Confidence

Many pupils lack the confidence to get things done. They believe they are not good enough, or will fail or just don't know how. This fun, creative activity begins a conversation about what is needed to boost confidence in the classroom.

A RECIPE FOR A CONFIDENCE CAKE

Teachers and/or pupils complete this activity in small groups. They are asked to think of ingredients and how they would bake a confidence cake. Confidence is connected with resilience – being able to pull yourself up when things have gone wrong. Many groups have completed this activity and although all the cakes have been a bit different here is an example of what has been included.

Ingredients:

- A rocky road base of resilience!
- Self-raising relationship flour
- Belief – believing you can, others believing you can
- Eggs of encouragement, support and guidance
- Have-a-go honeycomb
- A pinch of persistence
- A handful of help-seeking
- A big bunch of belonging
- Shake in a few affirmations
- Adventures and experiments and risk-taking
- Mistakes accepted as part of learning
- Lots of practice
- Mastering things in small steps
- Success experiences
- Positive and realistic feedback
- Accepting differences and celebrating individuality
- Hearts full of humour
- Toolbox of skills

Method

Start with relationship flour and belief, whisk in the eggs of encouragement. Add all other ingredients and mix well. Place in a warm, loving, safe place and bake slowly. Check from time to time to see how it's doing.

Decorate with 'I can do it' icing, sprinkle with smiles. Finish off with candles of hope and courage.

Teaching a routine

There are many routines in a primary school day, such as coming in each morning, lining up, beginning a lesson. Sometimes it helps to teach these and other expectations directly and give opportunities for practice. This is likely to save time later and will encourage children to remind each other what they are expected to do.

1 Gain the attention of all the pupils. Do this in a fun way. Fingers on noses works well. The children know that when they see you put your finger on your nose and your hand in the air then they do the same – and stop talking. Within seconds everyone will be quiet and looking at you. Saying that the last person to do this snorts like a pig is an added incentive and gives everyone a laugh!
2 Ensure that those who have most difficult paying attention are nearest you.
3 Explain carefully and simply what you want to the children to do (using visual supports if available).
4 Tell them HOW you expect them to do it.
5 Demonstrate to the children what you have asked them to do – children learn by watching and copying those around them – make sure it is you they copy!
6 It may be necessary to break the routine into small steps.
7 Give the pupils opportunities to practice.
8 Discuss with the pupils how they got on, giving positive feedback.
9 Remind the children of expectations each time they carry out a routine until they can do this without prompting.
10 Withdraw prompts gradually but continue to comment positively on how well they can do this.
11 Give reminders before reprimands.
12 Use the children's knowledge and skills to help a new entrant learn routines.

The problem: inattention

The recipe: listening and following instructions

What you need to know

Hearing levels: Many children below the age of seven have intermittent conductive hearing loss and although they can hear sounds they may not be able to make out the meaning of what is being said, especially in a noisy classroom. Check what they can hear when facing you compared to when they are looking away. NB: hearing gets worse when they have a cold.

Language skills: Does the child understand what is being asked? Young children may come to school without having had much in the way of interactive conversation so their vocabulary is limited. This is especially important if the child's first language is not English.

Attention skills: Does the child have dual attention channels? Can they listen and do things at the same time or not?

Too much information: Does the child listen at first but then switch off? Do they start working, then stop? Memory difficulties can include: short term memory (immediate); working memory (working with two or more pieces of information); or long term memory (e.g. connecting what they are doing now to what was taught last week). Might there be a need to give shorter or fewer directions at a time, repeat, summarize or paraphrase?

Strengths: When does the child listen best? What time of day, any specific activities?

Ability level: Is the child able to do what they are being asked to do?

At home: What have the parents noticed about their child and their ability to listen? Have they got strategies to share? Are there concerns about developmental milestones?

Today in the classroom

With the whole class:

- When giving instructions ensure the light is not behind you.
- Give short, clear instructions with visual cues where possible.

- Use names for the children you need to re-focus but otherwise do not single out.
- *Paula Pane
- *Proximity praise

With this child:

- Have the child sit near you.
- Ask them to look at you so they can lip-read if necessary – some children find eye-contact either challenging or culturally conflicting so ask them to look at your mouth.
- Give one instruction at a time and ask them to tell you what they are going to do in their own words.
- Make sure they know what it means to have 'finished' that task.
- Say you will come back to see how they are doing (*take-up time).
- When you return give positive feedback for anything completed and ask for *feelings feedback.
- If they have failed to do anything, ask them to complete a more familiar task so they experience a level of success.
- *Peer support
- *Visual cues

Longer term change

Differentiated learning so that tasks are at the right level.

*Structure success opportunities and praise effort.

*Circle Solutions activities to enhance listening skills, e.g. paired interview where children find out something about their partner and then feed back to the Circle.

Give attention to classroom layout and set up work stations with minimum distractions.

Build on anything that motivates or interests the child.

Provide visual support including charts of progress through a task.

For older children, self-monitoring with regular breaks may help. Ask them what they think they can manage and raise the time on task incrementally.

*Feelings feedback

*Personal bests

The problem: avoidance strategies

The recipe: focusing on directed tasks

This is where the pupil frequently engages in a range of avoidance strategies such as sharpening pencils or going to the toilet to avoid settling to work.

The aim is a student who is confident about beginning a task and motivated to stick with it. This behaviour is not uncommon for pupils who struggle with academic tasks.

What you need to know

Avoidance strategies: What is the student actually doing – does this give you any clues?

Which activities: Are there specific activities that the child avoids?

Situational clues: Does this happen in particular lessons, times of day, particular teachers, other pupils? When is the pupil most engaged, motivated and organized?

Equipment: Does the student have the equipment they need? If they have to bring it from home what are the issues here?

At home: Are there genuine toileting concerns?

Emotional cues: What does the pupil feel about the tasks they are being asked to do?

Today in the classroom

Ensure all materials needed are within easy reach.

Clarify *task priority and be clear about the very first thing to do.

Highlight key words or instructions.

Give *take up time.

Clarify times for toilet breaks to everyone – you may need to gently and privately remind the student to go at these times if this is an issue.

Give positive feedback for effort on any completion, however small.

Longer term change

Ensure all students understand what is involved in independent working. Give them a framework for beginning, continuing and finishing.

Build confidence by starting the student on familiar activities in which they have experienced success.

*Task analysis and checklist of steps.

Give students the following guidelines:

1   Do as much as you can yourself first.
2   Ask another student if you are not sure what to do next – *peer support.
3   If you're still stuck put your hand up to ask the teacher.

*Cooperative working with clear role for each member of the group.

Give responsibility for classroom tasks.

Have clear expectations of time on task alongside regular physical breaks.

*Traffic lights for needing to go to the toilet if this is an issue/excuse.

The problem: disorganization

The recipe: having the right things for a task and getting down to it

These strategies are for students who are disorganized and may be described as 'all over the place'. They need to learn to organize their belongings, their tasks, their time or all of these.

Being organized means:

- having what you need for a particular task (or lesson)
- knowing where things are kept
- understanding the importance of sequence and doing things in the right order
- knowing how to prioritize
- being able to manage time well rather than spending it all on one thing
- being independent and not relying on others.

What you need to know

When: Is this a problem in all contexts or just some?

What: Is the student struggling with time management, organization of equipment or organization of tasks? Or all of these?

Memory: Is memory a problem generally?

Sequencing: How skillful is the student in putting things in order?

Prioritizing: Can the student tell you the most important thing to do first?

Classroom layout: Can the pupil show you where everything is kept?

Putting things away: Does the student put things away in an agreed place when they are finished with them? Or is this haphazard?

Independence: Is the pupil used to other people doing everything for them?

Shared parenting: Are things in the other parent's house?

Today in the classroom

Ask all students to check equipment at the beginning of an activity.

*Proximity praise

Verbal and visual prompts

Longer term change

All students need to know the basics of good organization – independent working may need direct instruction.

Colour coded equipment may help.

Older students may need practice in setting out a task with its component parts and allocating time to each within the time allowed.

*Mnemonics

Work with parents so the student has visible reminders at home for what they need each day – perhaps pinned onto the inside of the front door.

Encourage use of lists with the pupil, constructing them in the first place then crossing things off.

Practice sequencing games to raise awareness of order. These could be simple to start with, such as what do you need to do when you are going for a swim/ make a cup of tea/have friends over to watch a film.

Give responsibility for aspects of classroom organization.

Teach and reinforce *routines.

Work with parents to increase independence.

See *Oliver and the Organization Owl* in the Wellbeing Stories (see **Resources and further reading**) for more ideas and whole class activities.

The problem: helplessness

The recipe: increasing independence

A student who says 'I can't' as their first response is either anxious about making a mistake or is used to other people doing things for them. It is possible they are not able to make sense of what is required. If a student is to work independently they need to feel confident to have a go in the first place and experience success, however small.

What you need to know

When: Does this happen with all tasks or just with some? When is the student most confident about starting something?

Circumstances: Does the pupil behave differently depending on whether tasks are individual, paired or in a small group? Does giving the student a choice or a task that matches their interest or strengths make a difference?

At home: What happens there? Is the pupil encouraged to be independent or is everything done for them? Are they given praise for attempting things even if they don't get it right? Might they get into trouble or be given negative messages about themselves if they don't succeed first time or take too long?

Ability: Does the student understand what they are being asked to do and have the skills to start?

Today in the classroom

*Task Analysis: Focus on the first step and link to prior knowledge/familiarity. Tell the pupil that the aim of this activity is to make a start and that is more important than getting it right – *mistakes as part of learning.

*'Take Two': Start the task with the pupil using the phrase '*We can do this*' and then give *take up time.

Help the pupil self-evaluate in terms of what they managed to achieve. Ask how they might build on this start next time?

Avoid giving too much attention that rewards the helpless stance.

Longer term change

Wall displays show that work of all levels and work in progress is valued.

Develop an *'I Can'* book, in which the student keeps records of all achievements. Work samples, photos etc. Share with parents and ask them for contributions.

Highlight student's achievements with others.

Use visual records/graphs etc. to show progress over time.

Student keeps records of *personal bests over a limited period of time.

Help the student make connections between effort, achievement and positive emotions – how do they feel when they do something independently?

In paired or small group *cooperative activities give the pupil a specific role.

Structure occasional opportunities for pupil to help younger children with specific tasks.

Work with parents to increase independence at home.

The problem: refusal to cooperate

The recipe: positive responses to teacher requests and directions

The student needs to feel *confident* (see earlier).

The relationship between the student and teacher is paramount.

What you need to know

Onset: Is this behaviour recent or entrenched?

Emotional triggers: Has anything happened at school or at home to increase anger or anxiety?

Purpose: Is refusal a way to maintain self-esteem? What does the student believe they will lose by co-operating?

Context: Is refusal across all subjects and all teachers or just some? When is the student most co-operative? What is the situation at home?

Confidence: Is behaviour linked to fear of failure? Have they experienced 'put-downs' for earlier attempts? Might they be avoiding potential negative emotions?

Today in the classroom

Be welcoming when the pupil comes into the classroom, smile, greet by name.

Calmly state expectations.

Give the task personal meaning for the child where possible.

Reassure that it is having a go that matters, not getting it right.

Give limited choices.

Clarify first thing to do and use *take up time.

*Tactical ignoring

*'Take Two' script: *'I can have go at that'*.

If this behaviour is unusual, talk with the student after the class to find out what is going on.

The pupil may not want to discuss anything – that is fine but leave channels of communication open and show care and concern.

If this behaviour has become habitual then it may take a range of strategies for it to change.

The pupil may need opportunities to get out of a corner – see *face-saving.

Longer term change

*Circle Solutions activities: Co-operative games. Focus on how students feel when they are working together.

Paired tasks.

Give the student leadership opportunities. Some defiance stems from a need for control so giving the student a role and responsibility can provide that in a planned way.

*Mistakes as part of learning

Reinforce co-operation by giving low key but specific positive feedback.

Promote positive self-image by structuring *success experiences in both academic and practical tasks.

Relate task to what the pupil finds meaningful.

*Strengths-based conversations

The problem: not settling but flitting between activities

The recipe: focusing on set task to completion

What you need to know

When: Does this happen with all tasks or just certain ones? Are these literacy (usually writing) or maths related?

What: What are they actually doing when flitting? Are they being distracted by inappropriate use of technology?

Which: Which activities does the pupil like doing and how long can they stay with these?

At home: Check what happens at home – is the child equally unsettled?

Environmental issues: Is the classroom noisy/distracting?

Anxiety issues: Is anything happening at home or in the playground that may be affecting concentration? It is likely that the pupil is anxious or uncertain how to proceed.

Today in the classroom

Clarifying *task priority may reduce anxiety.

Give small manageable steps with an incremental increase in the length of the steps.

Give several short-term tasks with a break in the middle of each. There is good evidence this increases focus and task completion.

Check that the pupil has everything they need.

Reinforce classroom expectations about technology as this may be a distractor.

Re-state expectations for task completion.

Praise small achievements and ask the pupil to reflect on how a completion makes them feel.

*Co-regulation

*Calming corner

Longer term change

Clarify expectations for moving around the classroom and when this is and is not acceptable.

Introduce the idea of task stages: planning, draft and final product.

Check that the pupil understands what you mean by 'finished' and introduce a 'finished' basket' for completed pieces of work. Students move onto the next task when they have finished the work in process.

Give different activities for the same learning goal.

Encourage self-monitoring – timers, checklists etc.

*Peer support and cooperative tasks

Discussion with families about encouraging talk about finishing tasks in stages – simple ones like getting ready for bed – talking about what happens first, then next until all steps are complete.

Also encourage focus at home e.g. staying with a meal until it is finished, watching a program from beginning to end. If the child gets up half way through the meal or starts something else when the program is on they have signaled the end and cannot restart. The child needs to know this is going to happen so has the choice.

Introduce mindfulness in the classroom.

The problem: distracted by others

The recipe: focus on set task

Some of the suggestions on similar issues about focus will also apply here.

What you need to know

Context: Does this happen in all lessons or only some? When are distractions least likely to occur? Are particular students the focus of the distraction? Are they encouraging this behaviour?

Relationships: What do you know about the pupil's relationships with their peers? How does this inform your intervention?

Today in the classroom

Re-locate the student away from any group that may be problematic.

Increase *cooperative activities – the pupil is less likely to be distracted if already working with others.

Ask the student where and how they feel they can work best.

Give positive feedback for focus.

Longer term change

Teach negotiation skills and provide scripts for all those who need to resist being interrupted, e.g.: *'I'm working now, talk to me later'*.

Give pupils opportunities to work collaboratively with a range of others in the class.

Promote class routines for different noise levels, illustrated with a 'noise ther-mometer' with a pointer to which level is acceptable for this lesson/activity.

*Traffic lights to give messages to other students:

- Red: Do not disturb.
- Amber: Just one question.
- Green: Open for conversation.

*Personal monitoring

The problem: starting but not finishing set work

The recipe: finishing assignments

What you need to know

Onset: Is this on-going or began recently – if the latter what has changed in the pupil's life? If it is on-going, is the work at the right level?

Context: Is this some assignments in some subjects or all? Is it classwork or home-work that is the problem – or both? If there are different means of recording does this make a difference?

Level: How much actually gets done? Is the problem doing too little or attempt-ing to do too much or redrafting over and over to get it perfect? Does the pupil rub things out or otherwise destroy work? What emotions are involved?

Today in the classroom

Be specific about what you mean by 'finished' and check with the student if they understand what they are expected to do. For example, five lines of writing, one page of maths problems, ten sentences with a verb.

Be explicit about marking criteria.

*Task priority

A checklist of steps towards completion

*Cooperative learning

Self-monitoring timing – ask the pupil what they think they can manage and set the timer for that time. It is best if they go for a very short time to begin with and then increase incrementally as the pupil achieves time on task. Encourage the student to keep a graph to show progress.

Longer term change

*Personal bests

*Task analysis with self-checking of steps achieved

Finished and unfinished work boxes

*Feelings feedback when they have achieved a target

Display student's finished work and work in progress

Whole class discussions followed up with individual reminders on:

- Planning work
- Drafts and redrafts
- Learning from mistakes
- Completion rather than perfection

For older students ask them to estimate how long each part of a task will take and set their watch to tell them when to go on to the next part. Review their estimates to help set priorities.

The problem: quiet disengagement

The recipe: building confidence

This behaviour makes few demands on teachers and can easily be overlooked. It is potentially linked with high levels of anxiety, so needs to be addressed gently.

What you need to know

Check the following:

- Language skills, especially receptive skills – does the student understand what is required?
- Sight and hearing
- Overall health, especially sleep
- Learning ability
- Prior knowledge
- Other situations at home or in school causing anxiety and loss of confidence.

At home: Is the family concerned? What does engage the child?

At school: What does the student engage with – how well do they do? Is the pupil engaged with other things at school, e.g. friends, sports etc.?

Today in the classroom

Ensure the pupil understands what they are expected to do.

Structure paired activities and give short term targets to both students.

Discuss afterwards how they did.

Give temporary access to the *calming corner so student can begin to learn to self-regulate.

Longer term change

Focus on slowly building confidence.

Show you have belief in the student and their ability.

Check what is meaningful and motivating for the student.

Structure *success experiences.

Use *traffic lights system to ask for help.

Address any medical/emotional/language concerns.

Section 2: dealing with disruption

© Elizabeth Stanley

Section 2: dealing with disruption

POSITIVE ATTENTION AND SELF-CONTROL

All children need attention. For some children, attention for negative behaviour is better than no attention at all. Others seek attention to distract from what they cannot do and/or are anxious about.

Some disruptive behaviours are the outcome of learning:

- Children who have learnt that negative attention has its own reward
- Children who have learnt they can achieve some status from peers by making them laugh or being outrageous
- Children who have not yet learned to control impulse
- Children who have not yet learned what is expected in a classroom.

Others behave in ways that are primarily self-protective. Pupils anxious about being faced with failure may take on the role of class clown. This is common with pupils who have average or above ability but struggle with reading and writing.

Diet

Some children have problems (also with settling to work) that may be linked to diet. Although the jury is still out, there is increasing evidence that refined sugar and some food additives contribute to uncontrolled behaviours. As well as reducing these foods it is also useful to increase consumption of what has been proved to stabilize mood swings, improve concentration and promote learning – the omega-3 fatty acids found in oily fish such as salmon and mackerel, together with walnuts, linseed, flaxseed and omega-enriched eggs. Increasing iron and zinc in the diet has also had promising results. Both pupils and teachers will be pleased to know that dark chocolate is a good source, as well as soy products, beans, spinach, raisins and shellfish.

Teaching and learning

The first ingredient in a strategy to address disruption is to teach expected behaviours. You do this by making expectations clear and then reinforcing the positive at every opportunity: *'thank you for . . . '*, *'I have noticed that . . . '*, *'Well done for . . . '*; Referring to *Paula Pane: *'Hey look, Paula, at everyone waiting quietly, have you ever seen such a well behaved class – I am SO proud of them.'*

Strengthen the positive

Some adults believe they will eliminate a behaviour by giving it the oxygen of attention and pointing out every misdemeanour. It simply doesn't work. This is why *tactical ignoring must always be balanced by positive reinforcement.

IMPULSE CONTROL

We live in an age of instant gratification, so it is not surprising when young people act on impulse. Lack of self-control is also regularly seen in the media. It is, however, a good idea to encourage children to control impulses from an early age, as acting without thinking may become a habit and cause more serious problems later on. Although this is the province of parents/carers it may fall to educators to fill in gaps. You may want to share the following ideas with families:

- Help children identify what they are feeling, teach them words for emotions and encourage them to use words rather than fists and feet to express themselves.
- Talk about self-control as a value – give it status.
- Teach problem-solving skills: children need to know there are alternatives in any situation and that they have choices. Ask them to identify all the options and then weigh up the pros and cons of each before they choose.
- Teach and encourage *breathing especially when emotions are running high.
- Be consistent so that situations/expectations are predictable.
- Ask children to repeat what you have said in their own words to check that they have understood what they are supposed to do.
- Rehearse less familiar situations to consider what might happen and how best to respond. Evidence suggests that children can manage social situations better when they have a chance to think things through beforehand.
- Model and talk about delayed gratification. You won't do/have something now for a more positive outcome later.
- Adults modelling healthy self-talk has been proved to have a positive impact on how children think.
- Talk about the gap between thinking and doing. How long does it need to be? Even counting to ten can work.

- Discuss what activities need a high level of control. Many sports do. Talk about what happens to players who lose control – and the impact on the game.
- Lively, impulsive children need many opportunities for physical activity – including those where there is an element of risk taking like adventure playgrounds, so they learn to judge what is safe.
- Provide opportunities for reflection and conversation on successful control strategies.
- Give positive feedback and identify self-control as a developing strength.
- Use a narrative approach that externalizes the problem. Encourage children to 'get those impulses to stay down' because it makes them feel better about themselves when they are in control rather than the impulse.

The problem: pushing or poking other children

The recipe: safe use of hands and feet

Children may need to raise their awareness of personal space and to establish contact appropriately with other children.

What you need to know

Context: When does this behaviour not appear – what is happening at these times?

Other children: Are the same pupils involved in this or is it anyone sitting near? If it is the same children are they encouraging this behaviour in any way?

Possible reasons: Check the following:

- Is there an element of revenge – is the child being excluded or otherwise bullied?
- Does the child want to make contact but does not know how to do this appropriately? Some children are deprived of positive touch and as this is an important aspect of healthy development will sometimes seek this out – even in unacceptable ways.
- Is the behaviour a distraction to alleviate perceived boredom? Is the pupil unable to sit still for more than a short period of time?

Today in the classroom

*Externalizing. Say to the student *'Your hands/feet are getting the better of you – how can you get them back in control? Show them who's boss!'*

Move the student near you or somewhere where there is less opportunity to poke others.

Give *The Look.

*Proximity praise

Use a reminder followed by a warning, then a *natural consequence. 1. *'Where are your hands supposed to be?'* 2. *'You need to keep them to yourself or you will have to sit somewhere away from other pupils.'* 3. Follow through.

Ask the class to stand and stretch or otherwise move for 30 seconds on a regular basis.

Give the student something to hold to occupy their hands.

Longer term change

Work with the whole class to remind them of expectations, such as hands in laps when on the carpet. This will differ depending on the age of the pupils.

Use a pre-arranged signal with the target child to both stop negative behaviours and give positive feedback for positive behaviour.

Teach *safe touch massages to the whole class and give children opportunities to practice. This has wider benefits as children are taught they can only touch someone with permission.

Another fun game is for children to do hand prints with this sentence stem: *'Hands are for . . .'* – and then showing hands carrying out this activity.

Circle sessions that ask children in pairs to talk about how to get someone's attention without yelling, poking or pushing in. Collate answers to display if this would help.

Hold PE sessions that raise the issue of control over different parts of the body.

Teach all children to put out their hand when they are being touched inappropriately and/or without permission and say loudly – *'Stop, I don't like that'*.

The problem: fidgeting, humming and other noises

The recipe: self-awareness and control

It is not natural for young children to keep still for long periods of time. When children are not allowed to roll over, stretch, hop on one foot, bend or bounce then the desire to move may become overwhelming and the least they can do is fidget! All children need to be up and out of their chairs at least once every half hour, even for only a couple of minutes. Apart from anything else it will stimulate their cognitive skills. Sometimes making noises has the same purpose as fidgeting. This may be annoying but also be part of normal behaviour. It is unlikely to be a deliberate ploy to disrupt or gain attention.

The aim here is to reduce the ways these behaviours impact negatively on others in the class and to check if they are indicative of other more serious concerns.

What you need to know

Context: In which situations do these behaviours happen most and least? What is happening at this time? Are other children involved?

Awareness: To what extent does the child appear aware of their behaviour? Is there any indication that this is a behaviour intended to be disruptive or has it become a habit? Is it perhaps an automatic response to situations where the child feels anxious? Can the pupil give a reason?

At home: What do parents say happens at home? What have they tried that is effective?

Physical issues: Is the child hungry or tired, as we all have less control at these times? Has hearing been checked? Does the child understand the language of instruction?

Other issues: Is the behaviour part of a wider cluster of behaviours that indicate more complex difficulties? This may include Tourette's syndrome.

Today in the classroom

Re-state expectations to the whole class for good listening and working. Using a few names including that of the child concerned when addressing the whole class may help to re-focus.

Ask questions to re-engage.

You may want to remind the class when there will be movement time. You may want to give the pupil permission to make noises at this time.

*Tactical ignoring – modelling this will encourage other pupils to do the same and not reinforce with laughter or attention. This is particularly important for random noises.

Quietly remind the child what they should be doing – ask them to tell you. Give positive feedback for compliance.

*Take up time

Longer term change

Rather than try and eliminate the behaviour, think about how to reduce it – and/or the level at which it disrupts others. Although fidget-spinners have been banned in some schools, they have a useful purpose. There are less obvious and quieter occupations for the hands, such as squeezy balls, doodle pads or worry beads.

Give the child as much control/agency as possible to increase *co-regulation. This could include choice of class seating to minimize others being disrupted, agreement on non-verbal signals as reminder of expectations or deciding on things they can fiddle with.

*Calming corner

The problem: attention-seeking silliness

The recipe: attention gained by positive behaviours

Silliness is defined here as behaviour that has no obvious purpose except to attract attention. It can include inappropriate remarks, wisecracks or slapstick. The student will need to learn positive behaviours that result in the desired attention. It is likely that any strategy will increase the unwanted behaviours in the short term. Keeping firmly to only paying attention to the positive will eventually work. Stay strong!

What you need to know

Context: Is attention sought from adults, peers or both?

Observations: What does the pupil actually do? Are they looking around to see the impact? Is the negative behaviour being reinforced by others?

Awareness: Is the pupil aware of what is and is not appropriate in a given situation?

Ability level: Is this work avoidance linked to performance anxiety? What are the student's competencies, especially in literacy? How do they see themselves in relation to others?

At home: What works for the pupil at home in gaining parental attention? Are there other things going on that help understand this behaviour – attention on another family member for instance? Are parents/carers anxious about poor performance?

Today in the classroom

*Tactical ignoring together with immediate attention for any positive behaviour

*Proximity praise

*The Look

*Strengths-based conversation

Longer term change

Have a private conversation with the student. For example, *'Tell me what you are thinking when you . . . '* or *'What are you hoping for?'* Keep the tone light and enquiring rather than critical. You want to know what might help the pupil not need such attention. Say you would like to work with them to get back on track. Also think about opportunities for legitimate showing off – such as a school play.

Work with families to provide positive attention. Help with scripts if necessary, e.g.:

- *Thank you for . . .*
- *I am proud of you for . . .*
- *I have noticed that . . .*
- *You are becoming. . .* (name strength)
- *I love the way you (make people laugh) but when is it OK to do that and when not?*

Work with the whole class using an agreed cue for everyone to ignore and not reinforce disruptive silliness. Engage students in a Circle activity to decide which behaviours this includes. This gives agency to the class, although must never focus on individuals. You might also want to discuss when it is fun to be silly and when not.

Be mindful of children with attachment difficulties. See **Resources and further reading**.

The problem: over-the-top behaviour

The recipe: measured responses

This is where a behaviour in itself is not inappropriate but its duration, frequency or level are inappropriate – and consequently disruptive. It may be that the child is just highly extrovert and demonstrative and has not yet learnt to recognize when this is unwelcome and tone down their behaviour.

What you need to know

Personality: Is extroversion a feature of the pupil's personality and valued by parents?

Onset: Has this behaviour begun or escalated recently? If so, has anything changed in the child's life?

History: If this has been chronic for a while, what has already been tried – and has anything had a positive impact?

Reasons: Is this a way of deliberately seeking attention or work avoidance (see previous problem)? Is the pupil unaware of what is appropriate for the classroom?

Hearing: Does the pupil speak too loudly because they have poor hearing? When was the last check?

Context: Are there particular triggers for this behaviour? People, place, time, subject?

Peers: Are other children encouraging or joining in?

Today in the classroom

Re-state expectations to everyone. Use *Paula Pane.

Place yourself near the pupil and if appropriate give *The Look or use a physical prompt when the behaviour begins. A gentle touch on the arm, shoulder or hand may be calming. Make this brief and stop immediately if there is any resistance.

Show belief in the pupil's ability to reassert self-control, e.g.: *'Brianna, you know what to do now, show me what you can do'*, and, for every small improvement: *'Hey, that's great Brianna, you are becoming . . .* (name strength)'.

If this does not work take the student quietly to one side and ask them to tell you why you are a bit concerned this morning/afternoon. Take the opportunity to remind them of expectations and ask them if they can monitor their behaviour for the rest of the day.

*Breathing

*Calming corner

Longer term change

Give the pupil opportunities to demonstrate strengths in positive ways.

*Circle Solutions activity:

Have several photographs that depict different situations and place them in the middle of the Circle, e.g. a football match, a courtroom, a library, a bowling alley, a cinema. Place pupils in groups of four and give each group one of the photos. They are asked to talk about what sort of behaviour would be expected in that situation and why. Ask them to think about noise, movement and interaction with others. Each group gives feedback.

The learning is for the whole class to think about what is appropriate and to understand that this changes in different situations. Use the learning from this activity in future conversations with the pupil.

*Personal monitoring

The problem: frequent interruptions

The recipe: waiting in turn

What you need to know

Learning: Is this a learnt behaviour reinforced by attention – either negative or positive? What happens at home?

Neurological issues: Does the pupil have problems with impulse control and is this consistent with other behaviours?

Patterns: Is there a pattern to the interruptions, e.g. to ask questions, to seek reassurance or to give information?

Context: When is this behaviour least and most challenging and what is happening at these times?

Self-concept: The pupil may think of themselves as not being able to control themselves but they will inevitably have self-control in some situations. Help them identify where and when and raise their pride in this.

Today in the classroom

Clarify expectations at the outset – including what to do if you get stuck.

*Tactical ignoring with attention when it appears that the student has been waiting well. Make a badge or label that says *'Not Now'* and just tap it without looking at the pupil.

Tape an agreed reminder to a desk.

*Proximity praise

Say *'Hands up please'*.

'I can't hear you' is for students who do not follow procedures such as raising their hand.

Longer term change

Give the student an agreed number of counters per week (or day). These are the number of times they can interrupt to ask a question or make a comment. Once they have used up their counters they will not be answered. You may like to give different colours for questions or giving information. This brings in another dimension to thinking. The number may need to go down as the student learns greater self-control.

Constant interruptions are unfair on others. It is like pushing into the front of a queue.

---

*Circle Solutions activity:

Give students in threes this situation: Four people were waiting for a bus. As the bus arrived a group of teenagers ran up and jumped on the bus ahead of the queue.

Students consider the following questions and give feedback to the Circle:

- Was this fair or unfair – what are your reasons for saying this?
- What do you think the young people might have been thinking?
- What if they were pushing in in front of someone you knew? How would that make you feel?
- Is someone interrupting all the time like pushing in front of a queue?
- How can we share attention fairly in this class?

The problem: outright defiance

The recipe: co-operation

The pupil may be desperate for some control in their life and apply this everywhere.

They may also need to learn that their sense of self-worth does not lie in winning every battle. Adults might need to learn this too!

What you need to know

Onset: Is this a recent behaviour or one that has escalated? If so, what has changed in the child's life?

Context: In which circumstances is this behaviour most problematic and what is going on then, and when is it least problematic and what is happening at those times?

Ability: Is it possible that the pupil is not able to do what is being asked of them?

Perception: Does the pupil not believe they can do what is being asked?

Loss of face: Do you have any idea why this behaviour makes sense to the student? Do they fear losing face in front of others?

Today in the classroom

Stay calm and do not take this behaviour personally.

Acknowledge to the pupil that you cannot 'make' them – or anyone else – do what you say. It is always their choice. However, each choice comes with *natural consequences. If they refuse to do something they will get further behind and that will not make them feel good about themselves. Do not threaten sanctions as this will just serve to escalate the situation.

Use I statements, such as '*I would like you to . . .* ' and not 'you' statements such as '*You should be . . .* '. I statements are much less threatening. Imagine a 'you' statement as wagging a finger in someone's face.

Show belief that the pupil will make a good choice and if possible link this to a strength.

Perhaps ask the student to just 'have a go' and then give *take up time.

Focus on your interactions with the rest of the class.

Longer term change

Have a one to one conversation that explores the student's rationale for the defiance. Wait until emotions have calmed down. Ask open-ended, curious and caring questions, such as *'What was going on there?' 'What was making you feel uncomfortable?' 'What could I do to help?'* Use a positive comment to begin the conversation and use this session to show concern, not reprimand. If the student refuses to speak, this indicates that they may be covering up the real concern. Perhaps suggest they draw or write what this is and bring this to you another time.

If the pupil was anxious about failure, point out previous successes. Give warning of more challenging tasks and emphasize effort rather than results. Ensure tasks match ability and/or ask students to work collaboratively.

The problem: rudeness

The recipe: courtesy/appropriate language

Rudeness is putting people down, using aggressive language, or a level of thoughtlessness that shows a lack of consideration for the feelings of others.

What you need to know

Specifics: Is it words, gestures and/or expressions?

Prior learning: Is this a learnt (copied) behaviour?

Level of concern: How serious is this? Is the rudeness escalating? Is it accompanied by other challenging behaviours?

Context: Is the rudeness directed at adults, peers or everyone? Is it supported by peers in any way?

Triggers: Is it a response to requests or more obvious at certain times, in particular situations or with specific people?

Today in the classroom

*Tactical ignoring for minor or brief indiscretions – but make your disapproval clear with the rest of the class by saying something briefly: '*Unacceptable behaviour, Rashid*'. If this continues, address after the class rather than give it attention.

Ask if the pupil intended to be rude and hurtful. Sometimes they do not realize how their words or expressions are perceived. If the student replies in the affirmative, ask what they wanted to happen. People who are intent on hurting others are usually feeling hurt themselves.

If the response is negative, ask if they know what it means to treat someone with respect.

If you are the target, state quietly that everyone needs to be treated with respect. Ask the student if they think you treat them with respect. It is possible the pupil is angry with others and finds people in school an easier target for their distress. If this is the case look at appropriate pages in **Section 4: emotional distress**.

Longer term change

The student needs to raise awareness of appropriate behaviour and this is best done in a group situation.

---

*Circle Solutions activities:

1: *Acronym Poem.* Mix pupils up so that they are in random groups of three. Give them a piece of A4 paper and ask them to write the word RESPECT down the side. They then think of a word or phrase to go with each letter, e.g. R – relationships, E – everyone matters etc. Each group shares their poem with the Circle.

   The learning outcome is that students begin to understand that in order to get respect you have to give it – and what this means in practice.

2: *Hello, good morning, how's it going bro?* Everyone wanders around the Circle and greets anyone they meet. The only difference is that they are told that the person they are meeting is either a family member, a teacher, a mate from school, their best friend, the receptionist at the doctor's surgery. Call out different roles as the pupils move around.

   At the end of this activity each student completes this sentence in the round: '*I learned* . . . '.

   The learning outcome is that students realize that how they speak to people will differ depending on the role that person has or the relationship they have with them.

Many children do not grow up using 'please' and 'thank you', so not saying these words is not necessarily 'rude'. If you think such courtesies improve class climate they may need to be actively modelled and taught.

Section 3: social interactions

Section 3: social interactions

Some children are quite well behaved in structured situations in the classroom but have difficulties relating well to peers in unstructured times of day and/or in the playground.

Feeling you belong is a critical component of wellbeing, so actively promoting inclusion in the classroom is a valid and sensible thing to do. Once this is in place many challenging social behaviours are likely to reduce.

In the first instance children learn social behaviour by watching, listening and copying. This means that the models provided by adults in school matter, not only in teacher–pupil interactions but also how teachers relate to each other. Students notice as this permeates the overall emotional climate.

Individual children who struggle socially need to be observed carefully as first impressions of their behaviour may not give the full picture. Sometimes the behaviour that is noticed is a reaction to provocation or rejection.

For interventions to be sustainable they need to take place within the context in which they occur and involve not just the teaching of skills but how children think about others. When progress is made within a class everyone can see and acknowledge this. You will therefore notice that many of the learning activities in this section are for the whole class group using the Circle Solutions principles described in **The oven: the emotional climate of the classroom**. For pupils who need more support, an intervention such as *Circle of Friends can be valuable.

How well people get on with each other is not only important for cooperative activity and promoting learning, it is also at the crux of much personal happiness or misery, both in childhood and later on. Positive, supportive relationships are also a significant protective factor for mental health and resilience. Children need to learn what is involved in establishing and maintaining positive relationships and how to respond when they get into difficulty.

Social and emotional learning is acknowledged not only as a pillar of wellbeing in schools but is also linked to significant behavioural and academic outcomes (see Durlak et al., 2011 in **Resources and further reading**).

The problem: not taking turns or sharing

The recipe: being fair

A pupil needs to understand that being fair is in their best interests.

What you need to know

Learning: Has the child learnt to share time or equipment in any situation? What happens then? Has any specific teaching on sharing taken place?

Issues: Are there specific difficulties for this child?

Emotions: Is the child anxious about sharing things they regard as theirs? Is there an evident reason for this?

Onset: For behaviour that has suddenly appeared, what has changed in the child's life?

Perceptions: How does the child understand the concept of fairness and how it applies to them as well as others?

Today in the classroom

Ask the student gently if they know what taking turns/sharing means. If they do, ask them to please show you now. If they do not then ask another student to demonstrate. You may want to add – *'now you have a go'*. Follow any success with congratulations for being a learner and a sharer.

Negotiate. For example, ask the student *'Do you need this?' 'How long do you need it?' 'When can someone else have it?'*

Re-state class expectations: *'In this class we all take turns, so you can have your turn and so can everyone else, . . . you have had your turn, who will be next?'* If the child does not respond say *'It is . . . 's turn now'*.

*'Take Two'

If resources are in short supply it may be that a clear system needs to be in place for sharing rather than leaving this up to individuals.

Use strengths-based language: *'I know you are a fair, kind person because I have seen you . . . so please show that you are being fair now'*.

*Proximity praise

*Paula Pane

Longer term change

Raise awareness by talking about fairness in everyday activities – e.g. borrowing books.

Give pupils practice in turn-taking games.

> *Circle Solutions activity:
>
> Mix students up and place them in groups of three. Have a number of scenarios with pictures that present potential classroom dilemmas, e.g. *'Liam has been playing on the bike for nearly all of playtime but won't give Ash a go even though she has been waiting and asking'*. The students are asked whether this situation is fair or unfair and what should happen. This means that all pupils are working on the same understanding of fairness and how to put this into practice.

Give the student responsibility for distribution of material/equipment.

Students who struggle with this may need practice in pairs before working in a small group and then the larger group.

Charts to show turns at various classroom activities, e.g. being a monitor, *star of the day.

The problem: bossiness – pushing in – wanting to be first

The recipe: appropriate assertiveness

The longer term change strategies below are not only for children who try to dominate but also those who are pushed around or silenced. Both need to know how to interact with appropriate assertiveness. Children who want to control others may need to feel important or included. They need to learn how to do this in ways that are respectful of others.

What you need to know

Observation: What is actually happening? If the pupil is trying to push into games, is this because they do not know how to join in or are other children being rejecting? Is the child trying to dominate interactions, i.e. change the rules in games? Might this be misplaced enthusiasm?

Competitiveness: Does the pupil feel the need to win in many situations?

Patterns: Does bossy/dominant behaviour happen in all interactions or only some?

Responses from others: How do other children currently respond?

Understanding: Does the pupil understand why games have rules? Do they understand that conversations and other situations also have rules?

Frequency: How often does this happen? Is it increasing or diminishing?

Learning: Is this the way the pupil has learnt to be or is it reactive behaviour in certain situations?

Other concerns: Is the child otherwise distressed?

Today in the classroom

*Strengths-based conversation. You may want to acknowledge enthusiasm but point out that it stops being a strength when it goes too far.

Distract the student, where possible, from any potential confrontation. Perhaps ask them to carry out a specific task away from others.

If conflict has occurred, acknowledge feelings and agree to meet with all those involved at the end of the lesson/session. Have a *restorative conversation.

Raise the pupil's awareness of their own behaviour: e.g. *'What would someone have to do to join in your game?'*, *'How would you feel if someone told you what to do all the time?'*, *'What would be fair here?'*

*Partial agreement, e.g. *'I understand you are upset about not being included in the game but pushing in like that doesn't help'*.

Encourage appropriate *assertiveness skills.

If the child pushes in to be first, reverse the order of the line – so those at the end go first.

Longer term change

Promote collaboration, *cooperative learning and teamwork rather than competition.

Focus on a *growth mindset. Praise effort rather than achievement.

Play games that have no winners and losers. De-brief about how much people enjoyed the game. Talk about the skills of winning well and losing well.

---

*Circle Solutions activities:

1: Mix pupils up and ask them to work in pairs or small groups to discuss the following: (This does not have to be all at the same time.)

- How would you ask to join in a game?
- How do you decide on the rules of a game?
- What would be a good way of responding when someone doesn't play properly?
- How would it feel to be left out of a game?
- What can we do to play well together in this class?

Put answers on the classroom wall so that they can be referred to when needed.

2: Present students with this scenario:
  Li wants to practice shooting baskets in the playground so he runs in and grabs the ball away from Jiang who is already using it.
  Jiang has three options:

  1 He can get very angry, yell and punch Li.
  2 He can just walk away and let Li get on with it.
  3 He can be 'appropriately assertive' and try a third way. Responses include stating what you feel and what you want to happen using an 'I statement'. You may want to add why and what you will now do. You won't always get what you want but this ensures that you don't get into trouble for hurting someone or get pushed around yourself.

Mix pupils up so that they are sitting next to a new person and ask them to say what will happen if Jiang chooses 1 or 2 and why being 'appropriately assertive' is a better response. After a few minutes pairs join up to be in a group of four and share their thoughts.

The problem: bullying and intimidation

The recipe: a safe and supportive classroom

Bullying behaviour can be verbal, physical or psychological – it can happen directly or indirectly on social media. This behaviour is defined as a deliberate and on-going attempt to undermine someone's positive sense of self and is often marked by a power imbalance. It can be perpetrated by individuals and also by a group. Others may collude by silence and inaction. Being bullied can have a long-term negative impact on wellbeing so this needs to be addressed at a whole school or whole class level beyond the brief suggestions made here. See also **The oven: the emotional climate of the classroom**.

What you need to know

Observation: What is actually happening and how often? Single incidents may be unpleasant and need addressing, but are not defined as bullying.

Recording: Much bullying behaviour is covert and there is little to see. Sometimes it is active exclusion of a child. Ask the children who are targets of this behaviour to keep a log of incidents – perhaps over a month. This both provides evidence and is also a way of raising their sense of control.

Exclusion: Are the incidents based on disrespect to someone because of their colour, race, religion, disability or gender?

Contexts: How does the pupil involved in bullying behave in other contexts?

Learning: To what extent might this be a learnt behaviour?

Other children: Who else is being affected? Do some children feel intimidated in case they are they are the next target? Are others actively joining in or feeling uncomfortable because they do not know how to intervene safely?

Today in the classroom

When bullying behaviour is seen taking place, the perpetrator needs to be told this is unacceptable in this school. Do not accept excuses, including minimizing, e.g.: *'it was only a joke'*. Do not force an apology, but arrange to meet with students involved later in the day. All pupils need to see that this behaviour is taken seriously.

See both students together away from the class. Have a strengths-based conversation with the perpetrator. Begin by pointing out their positive observable qualities, e.g. *'You have real leadership qualities, you can be supportive, encouraging and kind – I have seen you (cite observation). Would you agree? So, what are you telling people about yourself by behaving like this? What sort of person do you want to become?'*

Then use a *restorative conferencing approach that includes how the perpetrator can use their strengths positively to support/protect/show respect to/include the person they have been bullying.

Longer term change

As someone with authority the teacher needs to demonstrate respectful leadership and treat all students fairly.

Give the perpetrator a leadership role. Tell them that a true leader doesn't order people about but helps them be the best they can be. Monitor how they are implementing this. Check how this makes them feel about themselves.

Give responsibility to the whole class to ensure that everyone is included and feels safe.

These activities need to take place over several weeks to maintain the focus.

---

*Circle Solutions activities:

Bullying Definition and Feelings:

Mix everyone up using 'silent statements' – ask pupils to change places if: they know someone who is being bullied; they think bullying should be stopped; they are prepared to join others to take action to stop bullying.

Ask pupils in pairs to discuss the following and then give feedback together.

* *Being bullied would make someone feel . . .*
* *Watching someone being bullied might make someone feel . . .*
* *Someone who bullies others is trying to . . .*

Now work in groups of three to talk about what sorts of things can be described as bullying.

Upstanding:

Mix students up again and ask them to work in groups of three. They are asked to say what they can do to stand up for someone who is being bullied. There are relevant YouTube clips in **Resources and further reading** you may wish to use.

Class responsibility for inclusion:

Mix students up and divide them into groups of four.

A pupil (or teacher) reads out the following: *My name is Isaac. I was born with a large red mark over my face. Some people in this school think it's fun to say things like: 'Here comes the traffic light!' They just laugh at me. Sometimes other children won't play with me or go 'ugh' when they go past me. I hate coming to school.*

Ask students to answer the following questions:

- *How would you feel if you were Isaac?*
- *Is it his fault he looks different from other children?*
- *Why are some pupils so cruel to Isaac – or any other child who is a bit different?*
- *Are any of those reasons acceptable?*
- *What would you want to happen if you were Isaac?*
- *What will this group do to make sure everyone in this class is treated with kindness?*

The pupils are asked to write four sentences beginning: *'We will . . .'.*

Everyone in the group takes a turn to say one of these sentences around the Circle.

The teacher then collates these and returns them to the Circle another day.

As the teacher reads out each sentence, pupils are asked to change seats if they agree.

This is then written up and displayed on the wall as the class charter. The pupils can choose a title for this.

Other scenarios can be written for other types of bullying. The aim is to raise awareness, limit collusion, give children strategies to actively oppose bullying when it occurs and to promote responsibility for a positive and safe class climate.

The problem: fighting

The recipe: conflict management

What you need to know

Context: Which students are involved? Is it always the same group?

Frequency: How often does this happen – is it increasing or decreasing?

Triggers: Is there a pattern to the triggers for fighting?

Understanding: Does the child know when rough and tumble play gets out of hand?

Other issues: Is the fight equal or clearly down to the behaviour of one of the combatants? If the latter, is this part of a cluster of other behaviours? See **Section 4: emotional distress**.

Today in the classroom

Give firm directions to the child most likely to comply. Use the child's name (ask another pupil to tell you if you do not know), and firmly ask them to take action, e.g. *'Max, stand over here please'*.

It is much easier to respond to a request to do something than to stop something.

State very clearly: *'Fighting is not allowed in this school. We sort things out by talking'*.

Keep calm and raise your voice only if there is an immediate safety issue.

Avoid seeking explanations from pupils until everything has calmed down.

Move students to a place away from others and ask them to let you know when they have calmed down and are ready to talk. If matters are still volatile you may need to place them away from each other. If they have had any *conflict resolution or peer mediation training you may want to see if they can sort things out themselves, or with the help of another student. Otherwise, when they are ready use a *restorative conference approach.

Longer term change

*Circle Solutions activity on anger:

Mix students up and then place them into groups of three or four. They are asked to discuss the following questions (possibly not at once) and write down their answers to feed back to the Circle:

- What might make someone angry?
- Can you think of anything good about anger?
- What does anger make someone feel like inside?
- Why is hurting people not OK?
- What could someone do when they start to feel angry?
- What ways are there to express anger safely?

*Circle Solutions activity on conflict management:

Read this scenario out to the whole Circle:

> Jack is already upset. He had a row with his step-dad before coming to school and is ready to punch anyone who gets in his way. Leo, usually Jack's friend, doesn't know this when he teases him about his new hair-cut. Jack swears at him, Leo swears back and Jack lashes out. It becomes a full-on fight.

Mix students up by asking them to stand up and change places if they think this fight was Jack's fault, then if it was Leo's fault, and finally if it was the fault of both boys so both should sort it out. Say they can change places more than once. Now pupils work in pairs, one imagining they are Jack and the other Leo. They take it in turns to talk about what they would have felt, what they wished had happened differently and what they might want to happen now.

Now pairs talk about the 'Stopping Places' where this situation could have been handled differently so that it didn't escalate.

Each pair discusses what they learned during this activity and feeds back to the Circle: 'We learned . . .'.

The problem: stealing

The recipe: being trustworthy

The pupil needs to understand that taking things from others damages their reputation, chance of friendship and belonging.

What you need to know

Onset: Has this started recently, and if so what has changed in the child's life? In particular, has the student experienced a loss?

Patterns: What does the pupil take? From whom? When? Is there a pattern that gives information as to the child's needs? Are there other behaviours of concern?

Motivation: Is there a clear motivation? Is the stealing covert or overt? Is there any evidence that the pupil actually needs the things that are being taken?

Responses: What happens when the student is confronted? What do they say?

Level of understanding: Does the pupil know that what they are doing is wrong? Are they able to empathize with another person's loss?

Today in the classroom

Check first whether things have been borrowed without permission and make it clear that asking someone first is necessary and respectful.
   Gently but firmly re-state expectations depending on what is stolen:

   'You cannot take things that belong to other people. It hurts them and we don't want anyone hurt in this classroom.'
   'You cannot take things from the classroom – everyone here needs them so it isn't fair.'

Ask the pupil to return the things that have been taken. It may be best to find a way to do this that avoids the child losing face. A general amnesty might be an idea. It is likely that this child is not the only one to have taken things.

Ask the student privately if they can tell you why taking things that don't belong to them is wrong.

Use a *restorative approach with specific incidents if other children are involved.

(For **denial of responsibility**, see the next recipe.)

Longer term change

---

*Circle Solutions activities on the value and practice of trust:

Mix pupils up by asking them to change places if they agree with the following:

- A friend is someone you can play with.
- A friend is someone you can talk to.
- A friend is someone you can trust.

Students work in pairs to talk about what trust means. They find ways to finish these sentences – each person in the pair says one of these to the Circle:

- *'You know you can trust someone when . . .'*
- *'We show we can be trusted by . . .'*

When trust walked in

   Mix students up again by asking them to change places if they agree with these sentences:

- Being trusted makes you feel good about yourself.
- Being able to trust people makes you feel safe.
- Not being honest would make someone worried about being found out.

Students work in groups of four to talk about Trust both as a quality and as an action. They are asked to imagine what they would notice if Trust walked into their classroom one morning. What would they *see*, what would they *hear*, what would everyone be *feeling*, what would people be *thinking*? Pupils record their thoughts (perhaps with illustrations) on a large piece of paper and then share with others.

Use these activities and their outcomes to address any further issues. Point out to the child that not being trustworthy will mean that people will not want to be friends with them – this is a natural consequence. Further punishment is unlikely to be effective.

If the child continues to steal then this requires more intensive intervention, such as *Circle of Friends or counselling sessions. If appropriate, involve the family in helping you promote honesty and trust in the class in order to reinforce these values.

The problem: lying and blaming others

The recipe: accepting responsibility

What you need to know

Understanding: Does the student know the difference between truth, lies and fantasy? Is there a maturity issue here? Has lying become habitual?

Patterns: What does the pupil lie about? Are they more likely to tell the truth under some circumstances or with some people?

Rationale: Is this fear of punishment or losing face? Does the child want to please/ be accepted by others by 'pretending'?

Experience: Does the child have a history of getting into trouble for making mistakes?

Positives: Does the child accept praise/responsibility for positive effort/ outcomes/achievements?

Other concerns: Is this one of several concerning behaviours?

Today in the classroom

*Tactically ignore and do not engage in arguments with an audience.

*Partial agreement e.g. *'Maybe you didn't spill the paint but I do want you to help clear it up. We are all responsible for keeping the classroom clean and tidy'. 'Maybe you didn't mean to take Megan's pencil case but you need to return it to her now.'*

Use the 'responsibility pie chart' once children understand how this works.

Longer term change

Use strengths-based language and acknowledge when the child is truthful. Do not risk negative labelling which embeds a self-concept which does not discourage this behaviour.

The responsibility pie chart – divide the pie between these three:

- When a person always blames themselves when things go wrong, they end up feeling like they are useless or bad people and this can lead to depression.
- When someone always blames another person they feel exonerated in the short term, but then believe that they have no control over what happens, and this doesn't make them feel good either.
- Many things are also down to chance or are just accidents.

When something happens in the classroom you can ask the pupil(s) involved to think about what they could have done differently, what could someone else have done differently and what was just chance. This supports the appropriate taking of responsibility. You can also use this for positive outcomes, e.g. passing a test. Some of this could be down to the pupil's hard work, some perhaps to good teaching, some to parental support and maybe some to getting lucky with the questions!

*Mistakes as part of learning

The problem: cheating

The recipe: self-reliance

Cheating is more likely to happen when there is a strong competitive culture and some individuals are seen as 'successful' and others as 'losers'. Children who fear 'being a loser' may use all means at their disposal to be 'a winner'. This includes breaking the rules to secure an advantage, copying the work of others or passing something off as your own work when it isn't.

What you need to know

Observation: What exactly can you see happening? Is the cheating mostly overt or secretive? If secretive, what is the reaction when discovered? Does this upset other students?

Frequency: How often does this happen?

Understanding: Does the pupil understand what it means to cheat? Do they understand how this affects others?

Ability: Are they able to see themselves as successful learners without cheating?

Today in the classroom

*The Look followed by moving towards the student so they know you are aware.

Use *natural consequences when cheating is discovered. Where possible give the pupil the opportunity to repeat the activity without cheating.

Stopping a game and asking pupils to say why we have rules and what happens to the game when these are broken. Use sporting analogies that students are familiar with.

Longer term change

Ask students to work in pairs to say whether the following counts as cheating or not:

- Doing an assignment with someone else
- Copying a piece of work word for word from the internet
- Changing a rule to suit yourself
- Being dishonest so someone loses out
- Taking the credit when someone else has done all the work
- Asking someone for help when you get stuck

Ask if they can think of anything else.

Have a class discussion about the above, and:

- In what ways does cheating affect the people involved?

Reduce the levels of competition in the class and introduce a culture of *personal bests.

Increase collaborative and *co-operative working regimes.

Focus on a *growth mindset and give positive feedback for effort.

*Mistakes as part of learning

Ensure the student regularly has experiences that maintain a positive sense of self.

The problem: trying to buy friendship

The recipe: positive approaches to friendship

This may be indicative of a young person's desperate need for friendship or an inappropriate use of gift giving. The intention matters for determining intervention.

The student may need to develop and practice a repertoire of skills to establish and maintain friendship, and the rest of the class may need to practice being receptive and inclusive.

What you need to know

Observation: What are the social issues in the class? Are there cliques and rejected children? Is the pupil targeting specific children? Why these? Where do the items come from? Are parents aware?

Ability: Is the child less socially mature than others of the same age? Does this apply to other areas of development?

Competencies: What friendship skills does the pupil already have?

Perception: What does the child think about giving presents? Is this misplaced generosity?

Today in the classroom

Talk with the pupil to clarify their perspective and underlying reasons for giving presents – why are they doing this?

Talk with other pupils about not accepting presents unless for a special occasion.

Remove any valuable items for safe-keeping.

Highlight the student's strength of generosity but point out that friendship is about reciprocity and should not be one-way.

Longer term change

A school policy on related issues may be helpful. This could include what is permissible or not to bring to school, the value and practice of an inclusive culture and the importance of teaching and learning friendliness.

It may be useful to raise the tricky issue of parties with all parents/carers at the outset of the school year. You do not want to dictate who is invited but singling an individual out for exclusion is a form of bullying and can have repercussions in school.

There are many activities that support the learning of friendship skills and belonging in the school. This should include activities that focus on pupils talking together on issues such as *'What makes a good friend?', 'What can we all do to make sure everyone feels welcome?', 'What is fair in friendship?'*

The problem: everyone is against me

The recipe: acknowledging the positive

Some children have had experiences that have shifted their perceptions of others as 'out to get me'. It may take some time for a pupil to establish a more positive outlook, but it is important to help them do this, as it may otherwise turn into a paranoid approach to life which can impact on mental health. This has to be a two-way process that helps the student feel confident they are a valued member of the class and to begin to notice the positive.

What you need to know

Observation: How does this perception manifest itself in everyday interactions? Are particular children overtly negative – and are some positive? Does the pupil misinterpret what could be friendly approaches?

History: What do you know about how this perception developed? Is it getting worse or better?

Other concerns: Is this part of a wider pattern of difficulties?

Today in the classroom

Acknowledge feelings, even if you believe these are misplaced.

Ask *'What makes you think that?'* and offer alternative explanations.

Point out that everyone 'reads minds' sometimes and jumps to the wrong conclusions.

Remind the student of previous positive incidents.

Explain that sometimes people don't like what someone does, but it doesn't mean they don't like them.

Ask the pupil if they can tell you what behaviours other children might not like or want to avoid.

Longer term change

Comment to others (so the student can hear) about their strengths/achievements.

Say directly to them '*I have noticed that . . .*', and point out positive behaviours or friendly overtures from others.

---

*Circle Solutions activities:

Regularly mixing pupils up and doing paired interviews or pair-shares is a way of breaking down barriers and helping children get to know each other.
   Paired interviews are where children interview each other, e.g. 'What did you do at the weekend?', 'What is your favourite TV program?', 'What is the most you have ever walked?'
   Pair-shares are finding things in common. What do we both love/hate to eat? What makes us both feel better when we have been upset? What do we both like to play?
   Mix students up by asking them to change places if:

• They have thanked someone today
• They have included someone in a game this week
• They can change places smiling and hopping at the same time!

Now students work with the person sitting next to them.

Strengths identification

1   Spread Strengths cards on the floor, and each student in a pair chooses a strength they can see in the other person and then tells them why they have picked this.
2   Each student in the pair chooses a strength they want to work on this week. They meet up for five minutes at the end of the day to discuss how they are doing and what they have done to show this strength. The pair keep a notebook that they share with others at the next Circle session.

Friendship: Ask students to complete this sentence: '*We can be friendly in the class by . . .*'.
   Gratitude: Form two concentric Circles, the inner one facing out and the outer one facing in. The students on the outside move three places to the right so they are facing someone different. They have one minute to say something they are thankful for, then the outer Circle moves to the left three places to repeat the activity – and then once more.
   A further activity is for each person in the Circle to turn to the person on their left and say. . . *I would like to thank you for* . . . . Children need to be primed to be on the lookout for the positives in each other before this activity takes place.

---

*Star of the day

Section 4: emotional distress

Section 4: emotional distress

This section deals primarily with emotional distress caused by the following:

- Loss: this covers bereavement of loved family members and friends – including pets – but also includes family breakdown and long-term absence of a parent
- Challenging life events such as newly blended families, witnessing violence, caring responsibilities
- Unmet needs for warmth and acceptance
- Failure
- Real and perceived rejection
- Pressure to perform.

More complex distress caused by trauma is addressed in the next section.

All the events above can result in pupils feeling confused, angry, anxious, depressed and/or out of control. Sometimes these emotions make sense to the child but often they may not realize, let alone articulate, why they feel so bad. Although teachers may not know why a pupil is behaving in the way they are, there will always be a reason. It is not, however, necessary to know the details to be able to respond in effective ways. Rather than use valuable energy on things we cannot change, it makes sense to act on what is within our sphere of control.

Family breakdown is one of the most common reasons that children act out in school. It is significantly underrated. How a pupil reacts will depend on their age and stage of development and what they have been told at home. Those under 7 years old will invariably think that the disappearance of a parent is somehow their fault and position themselves as 'bad' – especially if the situation has not been mediated so they understand that they are not to blame. Such children may also behave exceptionally well at home for fear the other parent will also leave. The only place they have left for expressing their distress is in the safe confines of school. Re-constituted (blended) families with step-parents can be a blessing to many children, but adapting to a new regime and sharing your parent with someone else can be a real challenge for some individuals who need time and support to adjust.

Ask your educational psychology service or school counsellor to provide regular input for all parents on issues involved in family changes, and how these may impact on children and what they can do at home to help. This may help children where it matters most and reduce incidents in school.

Teachers may be at a loss to know what to do for the best when children express strong emotions, as it is likely to trigger negative feelings in themselves. It is particularly challenging to find the balance between supporting the pupil who appears out of control and containing the de-stabilizing effect of this behaviour on the rest of the class. Acknowledging the feelings being expressed is a useful first strategy. Once a child feels they have been 'heard', they are more likely to calm down sooner. Taking a pupil's behaviour personally is both exhausting and unhelpful. Emotions are very contagious, so it is tempting to respond to anger with anger. However, when adults behave with calm and control they provide a model for children to copy.

It is worth mentioning the role of the amygdala. This small almond shaped organ in the limbic system of the brain has the function of responding to a perceived threat. It fires off messages to prepare the body for fight, flight or freeze. This threat is not only to physical safety but also to a positive sense of self. If someone perceives themselves as being undermined, rejected or intimidated, their amygdala will rapidly go into action. As part of this reaction the neo-cortex is temporarily shut down, so they lose the ability to think straight for a while. It is wise to avoid asking 'why?' questions, as the emotion flooding the child's system makes them unable to answer. Invading their space in any way will be interpreted as a threat and make the situation worse. This includes a wagging finger, a head thrust forward, shouting or simply getting too close. Keeping your voice low and speaking slowly but firmly – asking the student to do something, rather to stop doing something – is more effective. You may want to suggest they go and have a drink of water or find a quiet spot away from others in order to give them time to recover from this 'amygdala moment'. Asking other pupils to go with them as support may also help. If you have trained peer mediators in your class, these would be ideal.

The *calming corner, and information on attachment in **Resources and further reading** will also be useful.

Raise awareness of emotions, emotional language, emotional triggers and the role of the amygdala with the whole class. There are some excellent clips to help with teaching children some basic neuroscience and the working of the brain in **Resources and further reading**.

It is hard to stay calm when a pupil is out of control and possibly abusive – so a whole-school focus on teacher wellbeing is a central ingredient in maintaining an effective response.

Individuals differ in their reactions to life events and this will depend on many interrelated factors, including how significant figures cope themselves and support children with difficult issues. Pupils who are emotionally volatile for a long time are likely to need more help. It is useful to keep a record of what has been tried, how long for and the extent to which anything has made a difference.

The problem: unprovoked aggression

The recipes:
1 To express strong feelings in ways that do not hurt others
2 To increase awareness of feelings to reduce acting on impulse

What you need to know

Onset: Is this behaviour recent or engrained? If recent, what has changed in the child's life?

Context: What do you know that triggers this behaviour? Is it at specific times of the day/week? With particular people?

Check: Is this behaviour actually unprovoked – are others involved? Is there a need for a social intervention?

Frequency: How often do incidents occur? Are these becoming more or less frequent?

Duration: How long do incidents last? Most of the time an incident will be momentary – it is more problematic if not. The answer to this will determine which of the following strategies you use.

Perception: What does the child have to say about what they hoped to achieve by this behaviour? This conversation needs to be at a time when no-one else is around and the pupil is calm.

Other concerns: Are there other worrying behaviours that need monitoring?

Today in the classroom

It may make sense to direct instructions to the pupil who is the target of aggression so they quickly move to safety. Say their name, followed by something like *'stand by me/leave the classroom'*.

To the child who is being aggressive: say their name followed by clear, firm instructions, e.g. *'hands on your head, please/move to me/fold your arms'* – whatever it takes to get the child to do something differently. It is easier to follow an instruction to *do* something than to *stop* doing something.

Do not invade the child's space by thrusting your face or fingers towards them. This will be interpreted as a threat. Speak in a low voice and slowly.

You may want to show belief in a child's ability to get back in control of themselves. If you have already built up a strong relationship this tactic may have traction, e.g. *'Come on Lucy, I know you can stop this, you can get back in control, I know you can'*.

Acknowledge feelings but say firmly that it is unacceptable for anyone in this class to hurt anyone else: *'No-one is allowed to hurt you'*. You may wish to ask the child if anyone is hurting them as their behaviour may be a reaction to this.

Making a child say sorry on the spot is rarely meaningful. *Restorative conferencing when things have calmed down is much more useful over the longer term even though it takes more time initially.

*Calming corner

A word about restraint. Although teachers are allowed to use 'reasonable' force, this is open to wide interpretation. Restraint is demeaning for a child and should be avoided at all costs. Try everything above, especially removing other children from danger. If you do have to restrain a child, do so as briefly and lightly as possible and say what you are doing as you are doing it. Record everything to inform future prevention. This is also a legal requirement.

Longer term change

*Traffic lights

---

*Circle Solutions activities – to be completed over several sessions:

Ask a pupil to volunteer to lie on the floor on a very large piece of paper. The teacher draws around their body, ending up with a life-sized shape with a head, body, arms and legs. Now mix pupils up by asking them to change places if:

- They have ever felt sad
- They have ever felt angry
- They have ever felt confused.

This 'silent statement' activity will show that these feelings are common to all.
  Now ask pupils to think about where in their body they might feel sad and come and put their initials on the drawn body in blue (leave the pens by the

drawing). Now ask them to do the same about feeling angry and put their initials in red. Now put confused in green.

The teacher draws in the amygdala and says that this picks up on anything that seems to be a threat and sends messages to all the other parts of the body to fight, freeze or flee. Give examples – if someone is unkind you might want to fight them, if you see a large spider you might want to run away, if a fierce looking dog is passing by you might want to freeze. Explain that the amygdala sends messages to your body that might make your heart race, increase your breathing and perhaps give you bursts of energy. Show this on the paper.

Ask pairs to think up things that might trigger the amygdala to go into action and make someone feel very angry. Ask them to feed this back to the Circle with a sentence completion: *'It might make someone angry if. . .'*

Everyone feels angry sometimes, but hurting people because you are angry never works out well and often gets you into trouble. Mix pairs up again by asking them to change places if:

- They like drawing
- They like writing stories
- They like running fast.

Give small groups several pieces of paper and ask them to think of how they can show their anger in ways that do not hurt people. Ask them to use the paper to draw or write what might help. Each group shows their work to the rest of the Circle.

Finally, ask groups to think of what they would like other people to do when they are feeling really upset and feed back to the Circle: *'When we are upset we would like other people to. . .'*

---

*Catch the child showing control and give positive feedback when they deal well with potentially challenging situations. Ask them if they feel good about being in charge of themselves.

If the student has several episodes of aggression in a day, set up a chart that records each hour/session/day they manage to stay in control. This provides visual motivation to maintain progress and gives the pupil agency.

Teach other children *appropriate assertiveness strategies.

See *Impulse control* in **Section 2: dealing with disruption**.

The problem: tantrums

The recipe: coping with frustration

The student needs to recognize what situations trigger strong feelings – including not getting what they want. Some young children will have been given everything they demand so will have to learn how to cope with frustration from scratch.

What you need to know

Triggers: What triggers tantrums?

Context: Do they occur at certain times/with particular people?

Duration: How long do they last?

Maintenance: Is there anything that keeps them going?

Family: What response do parents have? Might this need to change to help resolve issues at school? Are there other family issues that may be contributing?

Today in the classroom

What you do will depend on where the tantrum takes place, how it is expressed and the age of the pupil. Some of the suggestions below will be appropriate and others less so.

Ensure safety – remove hard objects from the vicinity if necessary.

Acknowledge distress, e.g. *'I can see you are really upset'*.

If acceptable (and only if), a light touch on the arm or shoulder may be calming.

*Permission: give the pupil permission to have the tantrum (you may need to encourage them to move to a less public place). Tell them to let you know when they are ready to talk and sort things out – this removes attention and can be effective in a short space of time.

Model calmness and control. This has two benefits: it shows the child that you are in charge of the situation, although not controlling them, and it gives them a mirror to copy.

Model and encourage deep breathing – this will help both of you.

*Saving face – sometimes children need a way out of a corner.

*Natural consequences, e.g. picking up anything that has been thrown or kicked over

*Calming corner

Longer term change

*Traffic lights

Knowing what triggers are may help with evasive, preventative action.

Check with the pupil about what they find upsetting – it may not be what seems obvious.

Work with parents/carers to develop a consistent response.

Raise awareness of strengths so the child begins to develop a more positive self-concept.

Discuss with the whole class that everyone gets angry and this sometimes helps us take action to put things right . . . but when anger takes over it can make things worse.

Use *Circle Solutions activities to raise awareness of what are safe expressions of anger and alternative ways of dealing with frustration. These could include: a cushion to punch to release energy, counting to ten and ten again (with deep breathing), problem-solving or walking away from a situation.

The problem: distress/tantrums/clinging when a parent leaves their child in class

The recipe: both child and parent are calm and comfortable

This situation is most likely to arise when a child first begins school. Most teachers know this is a temporary behaviour, but it can become an issue when it is persistent.

What you need to know

Child's understanding: What messages is the parent/carer giving the child about being at school? What messages is the parent/carer giving the child about how they will manage at home without them?

Child's development: Are there language/toileting/social or other issues that may impact on a successful transition?

Other concerns: Are there family issues that may be causing the child anxiety about leaving home?

Experience: What are the child's prior experiences of a nursery/playgroup/child-minder?

Today in the classroom

If a mother begins to be visibly upset, suggest a private place away from the child.

Reassure anxious parents that their child will be OK and tell them who they can talk to at school if they are worried. You may want to consider videoing a child to show them positively engaged in learning activities after their parent has left.

Have the equivalent of a 'security blanket' for the child. This could be a symbol drawn in felt pen on both the parent's and child's hand/a handkerchief sprayed with a familiar scent/a photo.

A 'worry doll' to talk to can be helpful for young children who are particularly anxious.

Plan a fun/distracting activity, possibly with another child.

*Co-regulation

Longer term change

Invite new children and their parents in before school begins so they can familiarize themselves with the place, the people and the resources.

Ask prospective parents to give the child positive messages about being in school.

Give parents a role and purpose in preparing their child for this important transition. This could include *strengths-based conversations related to independence.

Suggest the child has a good breakfast – hunger can exacerbate negative emotions.

Suggest parents do not engage in long drawn-out goodbyes each morning. Encourage them to smile and show enthusiasm where possible.

Encourage parents who are finding it difficult to leave their child to plan some activities for that day that are easier to do when child-free.

The problem: frequent or prolonged crying

The recipe: talking about difficulties/ feelings

What you need to know

Context: Does this happen in particular circumstances? Does it happen at home as well as at school?

Onset: Has this started recently? If so, what has changed in the child's life?

Triggers: Is there an evident trigger?

Frequency and duration: How long do the episodes last? Are they getting more or less frequent, longer or shorter?

What has helped: Has any intervention been effective, even minimally?

Does anything make it worse: Are there responses from either peers or adults that exacerbate or maintain the crying?

Today in the classroom

Acknowledge and validate feelings. Perhaps a comforting hand on the arm or shoulder may help. Take the lead from the child about this and ensure it happens in full view of others.

*Permission: let the child cry for as long as they need to and to let you know when they are ready to get on with other things. This combines empathy, agency and minimal attention. You may need to find an appropriate and comfortable place.

Give brief positive attention for being back in control and offer a familiar, calming activity.

Tell the child when you are available to listen when/if they are ready to talk.

*Calming corner

*Co-regulation

Longer term change

Provide opportunities for the pupil to confide in what is causing the distress. Do not exert pressure for information as this may be outside the child's comfort zone.

Schools often provide the stability and security that children lack elsewhere. Supportive relationships at school are a strong protective factor in resilience.

Work closely with families where appropriate.

Provide opportunities to express emotions in creative activities.

*Circle Solutions activities with the whole class to extend emotional vocabulary, promote empathy and explore ways to promote resilience.

'Externalizing' conversation: positioning the crying as getting in the way of what the pupil would really like to do.

The problem: destructive behaviour (own work)

The recipe: valuing personal efforts and achievements

What you need to know

Learning: Has the child learnt to value only what is perfect?

Purpose: Is the destruction linked to frustration? Is this because

- the pupil has not yet learnt the skills required so the level of work needs to change?
- there is misunderstanding about expectations?
- the pupil has overall low self-esteem?

Onset: Has this begun or gotten worse recently?

Frequency: How often does this happen?

Context: Does this happen with certain subjects? Is the pupil pleased with any achievement? What is this?

Other issues: What else might be contributing to or maintaining this behaviour?

Today in the classroom

Acknowledge feelings and give space to calm down – model slow, deep breathing.

Maintain a low-key response.

Clarify *task priority.

Ask the pupil to identify one benchmark for success.

Discussion of drafts: determine a maximum number of drafts and ask the pupil to choose their best attempt.

*Strengths-based conversation

*Personal best

Longer term change

Focus on *growth mind-sets with the whole class and with parents/carers.

*Mistakes as part of learning

Adults model acceptance of constructive criticism.

Involve student in displaying work of their choice.

Structure *success opportunities.

The problem: destructive behaviour (other people's work and possessions)

The recipe: treating belongings with respect

What you need to know

Frequency: How often does this happen?

Emotional content: Is it an angry, impulsive behaviour or secretive? Is it a reaction to rejection?

Context: Is there a pattern – times/people/places/triggers? In what circumstances is the pupil most calm and cooperative?

Responses: How do other children react?

Perception/motivation: Is there any indication what the pupil wants by behaving this way?

Contributing factors: Are there circumstances at home and/or school that are relevant?

Today in the classroom

Calm but clear, firm message that this behaviour is unacceptable – give attention to the child whose work has been damaged.

*Restorative approaches

Longer term change

*Circle Solutions activities:

Mix students up so they are working with those outside their usual social circle.

Ask them to discuss in pairs what they have made or done that they are proud of.

Ask someone to volunteer to read the following script:

My name is Morgan. I did a drawing I was very proud of, it took me ages. I went up to ask the teacher to come and look and when I came back someone had put red pen all over it.

Pupils work in groups of three. Ask the following questions one at a time. One of the group feeds back answers to the whole Circle again, one at a time. Point out similarities between groups.

- What would you be feeling if you were Morgan?
- Why might someone do this?
- Might this be a joke? Why is it not funny?
- What can we do to make sure everyone is kind to each other in this class?

Ask each group to come up with three actions. Collate ideas and display them on the classroom wall.

*Traffic lights to promote impulse control.

*Strengths-based conversations to develop a more positive self-concept.

The problem: selective mutism

The recipe: confidence in speaking

These children are usually able to speak in social situations where they feel safe, confident and relaxed, but are unable to communicate verbally in other settings such as school. It is a form of extreme social anxiety or phobia, and it is not within the child's gift to 'snap out of it'. It is important to recognize that this behaviour is not a choice. It is a 'freeze' response to threat. It is more common where there are other language difficulties, including English as an Additional Language, and often begins when a child starts school.

What you need to know

Context: With whom does the child feel most comfortable? Are there peers with whom the child interacts more readily? Is there anything at home or at school triggering/maintaining this level of anxiety? Are there observable differences between different contexts at school?

Learning: Is the pupil otherwise able and learning?

Other concerns: Are there other issues of concern? Isolation, other anxieties? Does the inability to speak give rise to other issues such as toileting issues, asking for help to complete assignments?

Strengths: Is the child they willing and able to communicate in ways other than speaking? Gestures, writing? Will they whisper a word or two? Does the child smile or laugh on occasions?

Today in the classroom

Have the same expectations for this pupil as for others with the exception of communication: i.e. treat them in terms of their strengths, so that they are not defined solely by their communication difficulties, and are not overlooked in a busy classroom.

Offer alternatives for communication but put no pressure on the child.

Have a warm but low-key response to any communication effort. You may want to echo what you heard if the child's voice is very quiet.

Verbalize what the child is doing, e.g. *'I see you are drawing a house'*.

Patience – ask simple questions and wait five seconds for an answer.

Longer term change

A positive emotional climate for learning will enable the student to feel more relaxed and supported.

The following intervention was very successful for a 7 year old girl. She met in a small group twice a week for 15 minutes. The group went through fun activities that built on a sequence of increasing communication. The criteria for moving onto the next stage was everyone contributing twice.

Level one: non-verbal games such as Simon says, Mexican wave, pass a smile.

Level two: single sound games, e.g. animal noises, transport noises. One example was giving pupils a picture of an animal, and asking them to find their pair with the same picture just by making noises.

Level three: single word games, e.g. picking up a symbols card that makes you think of something you like and saying what it is – lighthouse, star, book. I-Spy.

Level four: phrases, e.g. sentence completions.

Level five: inviting others into the group, holding the group in the normal class.

This could be segmented further by responses by the whole group, copying the teacher, paired activities and then individual ones.

---

*Circle Solutions activities with the whole class emphasizing the choice to remain silent also build social confidence.

The problem: disengagement

The recipe: participation/resilience

This section addresses the needs of students who seem very low and withdrawn.

What you need to know

Specifics: What is actually happening, or not happening? Is this just a quiet student or is this a problem? Not every child is an extrovert.

Basic needs: Is the child getting enough sleep, nutrition?

Medical/sensory information: Does the pupil have a reason for not engaging that is not primarily emotional, but physical or cognitive e.g. undiagnosed hearing loss, lack of understanding?

Social issues: Is the child being rejected or otherwise bullied by others and withdrawing as a consequence? Is there any peer support?

Onset: Is this recent, on-going or getting worse?

Context: Is the student equally disengaged in all contexts? Where and with whom is the pupil most engaged?

At home: Are parents/carers concerned? What happens at home? Are home circumstances contributing?

Today in the classroom

Offer limited choices rather than present open-ended decisions.

Maintain clear expectations for work and behaviour and comment on positive efforts.

*Strengths-based conversation

Longer term change

Engage the pupil in aspects of class maintenance.

Structure opportunities for collaborative work with supportive peers.

Work with the whole class on recognizing positive and negative self-talk (see Wellbeing Stories in **Resources and further reading**).

*Mindfulness with the whole class

Make it clear when you are available to listen should the student wish to talk.

Whole class activities that promote laughter – this both enhances a sense of connection and also relieves stress.

This situation needs careful monitoring if the pupil is at risk of deepening depression.

The problem: negativity

The recipe: positive re-framing

Negativity can be demonstrated in various ways including perceptions of others and their intentions, being overly self-critical and a focus on what is not going well. Trying to persuade someone out of their negativity is likely to be ineffective as is being negative yourself, so there needs to be a different approach altogether.

What you need to know

Onset: Is this habitual or more recent? If the latter, what may be contributing at school or at home?

Context: Are there specific issues where the pupil is more negative/sensitive?

Exceptions: Are there times/people/activities that elicit a more positive outlook?

Learning: Is negativity being modelled by significant people?

Impact: To what extent is this world view impacting on behaviour, learning and social interactions? Where is it most useful to intervene?

Today in the classroom

Acknowledge and validate feelings.

If possible, check what emotions underpin the negativity, e.g. fear of failure, being unsure about what to do, embarrassed, anxious about being excluded?

See if you can find a point of agreement so this becomes a shared issue – be specific.

State *'I wonder if we can find another way of seeing/thinking about this'*.

Positively reinforce any demonstration of positivity, problem-solving or personal strengths.

Longer term change

Notice positivity with all pupils.

Demonstrate optimism – belief in what they can do.

*Personal bests

Keep a journal for copies of good work, positive events and personal positive comments.

Raise awareness of self-talk – see Wellbeing Stories in **Resources and further reading**.

End of day *ticket out the door

*Star of the day

The problem: high levels of anxiety

The recipe: increased confidence

What you need to know

Specifics: Is this unfocused general anxiety or more specific, e.g. taking tests, harm to family members? How is the anxiety presented and how does this impact on what happens in the classroom? Are there psychosomatic symptoms – headaches, tummy ache etc.?

Exceptions: When does the student display most confidence? With whom? Doing what?

Triggers: Does low level anxiety become panic in certain situations? What triggers this?

Frequency: If so, how often does this happen? Is it getting better or worse?

At home: Are there changes at home that are contributing? Does the child have access to TV and social media that are increasing anxiety?

Expectations: What are the conversations about success and failure that may be contributing?

History: Has anything been tried in the past that has had a positive effect, even if small?

Today in the classroom

Acknowledge and validate feelings.

Reassurance needs to be specific, otherwise it may sound dismissive e.g. *'Remember the time when you were able to . . .'*

Do not single the pupil out.

Comment positively on effort and any achievement.

Use *strengths-based language where possible, e.g. *'I can see you are becoming more courageous'*.

Give warning of any changes in routine.

Give the student time to calm down when in a highly anxious state.

*Calming corner

*Co-regulation

Be aware of messages about assessments that may raise anxiety about performance.

Link new activities to more familiar ones.

Longer term change

Talk to the child about what they would find helpful when feeling anxious.

*Mistakes as part of learning

Regular relaxation activities with the whole class – reducing physical symptoms of stress. Simply standing and stretching for a couple of minutes has multiple benefits for all students.

---

*Circle Solutions activities:

Raising awareness of self-talk

Mix the class into groups of three. Give them the following phrases on separate pieces of card stock or paper. These are things we might say to ourselves. Ask students to place them in two piles according to whether they will increase confidence or raise anxiety.

I can have a go:
Everyone will laugh at me:
I can learn from mistakes:
Just do one thing and see how it goes:
It will be a disaster:
Where can I hide?
I will never learn:
Success begins with the first step:
I'm no good:

Take a chance:
I can't:
It's too hard:
I can do this!
Take a deep breath and try:

Making a confidence cake

Mix students up to work in groups of four. Give them a large piece of paper and felt pens.

Ask them to devise a recipe for a confidence cake. What would go into it, what ingredients would you need, how would you bake it, how might you decorate it? Encourage them to draw the cake. Each group displays their cake for others to see.

Use the findings from this activity to develop whole class strategies to build confidence.

See *William and the Worry Wart* in the Wellbeing Stories in **Resources and further reading**.

Section 5: behaviours of special concern

Section 2: behaviours of special concern

Section 5: behaviours of special concern

All behaviour is on a continuum from what might be expected for a child's age and stage of development and that which is not. Isolated incidents of unusual behaviour are not likely to be significant, but this section deals with behaviours outside the norm that are more severe, frequent or part of a pattern. These behaviours are often of special concern to teachers as they are confusing, sometimes bizarre and do not always respond to interventions that are effective in other circumstances. See the **Resources and further reading** and **Bibliography** sections for more information.

The behaviours that fall into this category include:

Medical conditions

Sometimes a child's behaviour changes with no apparent reason and appears to get more frequent or severe. This can include physical complaints such as frequent headaches, stomach aches and sickness, but also uncontrolled behaviours. Advise the parents to see their doctor to at least rule out neurological and other medical conditions.

Foetal alcohol syndrome (FAS)

This is often evident at birth and accompanied by low weight and slow development. It is not, however, always picked up early and there is a concern that more children have the neurological impairment caused by FAS than is often recognized. When the child goes to school they have difficulty with short-term memory, concentrating, learning and frustration. This can lead to behavioural difficulties. Sometimes there is an inappropriate diagnosis of ADHD or autism.

Autistic spectrum

This again is a broad continuum, from children who are cognitively able (occasionally with exceptional abilities) but have significant social comprehension difficulties and some unusual behaviours (Asperger's syndrome), to pupils who are struggling in all dimensions of their development and often need specialist support. There is greater awareness of autism now than previously, though it is still often the case that it is aberrant behaviour that alerts teachers that a child may be on the spectrum.

Autism can only be formally diagnosed by a paediatrician, but the following cluster of behaviours indicate that full assessment may be needed. If that is the case, it needs to be handled very sensitively with parents/carers who may experience a range of challenging emotions at the realization of the difficulty. Not every child on the autistic spectrum displays all of these, and they are all on a continuum from mild to severe:

- Lack of symbolic play, e.g. no make-believe scenarios with dolls or cars
- Repetitive behaviours – doing the same actions over and over again
- Self-stimulating behaviour such as flapping hands or head-banging
- Pre-occupation with a narrow field of interest
- Fascination with things like spinning objects
- Need for order, routine and fear of change
- Communication difficulties and delay
- Not understanding that other people have their own thoughts (theory of mind)
- Difficulty understanding other people's feelings or non-verbal cues
- Not looking at others or smiling in response
- Not being interested in others or in social interaction with them
- Sensory sensitivity – e.g. not being able to bear loud noises or being touched
- Echolalia – often repeating what others have said with no communicative intent
- Literal understanding – missing humour, metaphor or irony.

When struggling with some of the above or faced with particular challenges, children on the spectrum may display extreme behaviours such as screaming, hitting out or complete panic.

The suggestions made in this section may help but teachers need specialist advice for children on the autistic spectrum.

Trauma

Trauma is different from any other stressful situation, in that it is caused by situations that are outside normal experience, unpredictable and overwhelming. These could include witnessing violence or a bad accident, being involved in a natural disaster, physical or sexual abuse or otherwise being attacked or abandoned. Children who have been traumatized do not all respond in the same way. Circumstances of the situation are critical: who was involved, whether it was a single incident or ongoing, how significant others are coping and what else is going on in the child's life. Reactions may be immediate but are also delayed. More common indicators of trauma are:

- Hypervigilance – not being able to relax and appearing to be on the edge of panic

- Sleep difficulties
- Regression – reverting to behaviours of an earlier developmental stage
- Intrusive thoughts – sometimes children can react powerfully to something that reminds them of the incident, such as a smell, a sound or even a piece of clothing. They are not always able to articulate the trigger, so teachers may not know what has caused the outburst.
- Physical complaints
- Personality changes – e.g. from an outward child to a much more withdrawn one
- Recklessness
- Self-harm.

Sexual abuse

Child sexual abuse (CSA) is an extreme form of trauma, as it is usually perpetrated by someone the child depends on for care, is often ongoing and may be accompanied by threats. It destroys self-worth, trust and the ability to focus on learning. It often leads to serious mental health issues in the future. In addition to the above signs of trauma, the following may be an indication that the child is being abused:

- Complaints of soreness in the genital/anal areas
- Inappropriate sexual knowledge
- Sexualized play
- Fear or avoidance of certain adults
- Aggressive or withdrawn behaviour.

Evidence of abuse requires mandatory reporting.

MONITORING

It is important to carefully monitor and record incidents related to any of the above issues, so when you have conversations with colleagues, other professionals or parents you have evidence for your concerns. See **The team: family** at the beginning of this book so you can approach families in ways that will be perceived as supportive rather than accusatory.

TEACHER WELLBEING

This section addresses some of the behaviours that you may be faced with in the classroom that are linked to the above. Sometimes a pupil's behaviour and distress may be overwhelming. Your own wellbeing is paramount, as these concerns can undermine a sense of competency and in some cases can make a caring teacher feel helpless. Remember, you can only do what is within your circle of influence and you may be making more of a difference than you know. Seek support both in school and outside.

The problem: obsessive or ritualistic behaviour

The recipe: reduced anxiety and sense of control

This behaviour may be indicative of autism and also of trauma. It may also be neither of these, but linked to fear of failure/imperfection, and it can take many forms, from compulsive hand-washing to re-doing work over and over again, to repetitive actions to maintain a sense of safety.

What you need to know

Specifics: What exactly is the issue and how is this impeding learning or relationships?

Onset: Did this begin as a result of an incident or has it been gradual and on-going?

Frequency: Is the behaviour becoming more or less frequent?

Pattern: Is this part of a pattern of other related behaviours?

Perceptions: Is the pupil aware of their behaviour and does it distress them? Would they like to reduce their feelings of compulsion?

Context: Is this behaviour the same at school and at home? Are there additional stressors that exacerbate it? What are these?

Exceptions: Are there circumstances in which this behaviour is less frequent? Can you replicate any of these in the classroom?

Today in the classroom

Build in predictability and routine and give notice of any changes.

Give minimal attention.

Distract where possible with an alternative activity.

If the behaviour is being exacerbated by other stressors, remove what you can.

*Strengths-based conversation

Longer term change

If appropriate, initiate a problem-solving conversation that gives the child agency, e.g. ask what they could do instead, whether they could reduce the behaviour one step at a time and what would help?

*Externalize the issue – the compulsion is getting in the way, so how can we stop it from taking over the real you. Ask how they feel when they have taken control of a situation.

Ask *'what do you think would happen if you didn't do this?'* (sometimes children have magical thinking, e.g. *'if you step on the lines the bears will get you'*). You may not stop the behaviour but you can gently challenge it. Children may need to know that they are not responsible for chance events.

Raise awareness of inner discourse – negative thoughts that underpin the behaviour.

*Mistakes as part of learning, so children do not obsess over perfect work.

The problem: sexually explicit behaviour

The recipe: awareness of what is acceptable and safe

Consider first whether what is happening is normal developmental behaviour or something more worrying. Children will be curious about their bodies and will explore their own and maybe others'. There is very useful guidance on what is likely to be normal behaviour and what is more or very concerning at different ages from Forth Valley NHS Scotland. See **Resources and further reading**.

Behaviour that is indicative that the child is at risk will be either because they have seen pornography or otherwise witnessed sexual behaviours or been abused themselves. Responses need to be empathic but also ensure that others are not also put at risk. Record incidents of concern and follow notification procedures.

What you need to know

Specifics: What exactly is happening? This could be play scenarios, divulging detailed sexual knowledge to others, drawing pictures of genitals and/or sexual acts, public masturbation, exposure or behaving in a sexualized way with peers. NB: Children on the autistic spectrum may masturbate through lack of social awareness.

Onset: When did this start and is it in line with other indicators of concern?

Family: You may want to seek advice before raising your concerns with the family.

Today in the classroom

Stay calm and quiet so as not to draw attention to the behaviour or humiliate the child.

Shake your head and give a thumbs down.

Gently move the child away from others and tell them this not OK and a reason why not, depending on what has actually happened.

Direct them onto another activity or re-state what they should be doing.

If this has happened before, ask the child to tell you why this is not OK.

Be careful not to ask leading questions.

Longer term change

There needs to be a consistent whole school approach to responding to such behaviour so that pupils do not get mixed messages.

All children need educational input from an early age about keeping safe. See **Resources and further reading**.

Provide general family awareness sessions, so parents know what is not appropriate for children to access and how to monitor their screen use. You can also let them know about the child protection procedures that are followed at school.

The problem: soiling (encopresis) and smearing (scatolia)

The recipe: age appropriate self-care

It is easy to position soiling as deliberate, but jumping to conclusions could make an already sensitive situation worse. Soiling caused by incontinence may be very distressing for the child, as the resultant smell is likely to have negative social repercussions, like avoidance or bullying, as well as anxiety. It can also cause frustration and embarrassment for the family. When accompanied by smearing faeces it may have different connotations and meaning. This is recognized as a difficult behaviour to eradicate, so do not expect any quick fixes.

NB: Many young children have occasional 'accidents', mostly wetting their pants because they don't get to the toilet in time. This does need investigation if it becomes frequent, as it can be a sign of stress and anxiety.

What you need to know

Onset: Is this primary encopresis (continuous soiling – the child has never been toilet-trained) or secondary (started afterwards, possibly in conjunction with stress or trauma)?

Family: What has the family done so far? Have they sought medical advice?

Context: Are there stressors that exacerbate this behaviour or times when it diminishes?

Other concerns: Is this part of a pattern of other behaviours of concern? May this be linked to overall developmental delay or autism?

Emotions: What feelings are apparent in these behaviours? They may be linked with anger, a need for control, frustration, anxiety, fear, curiosity or even comfort.

Today in the classroom

Soiling: As soon as the behaviour becomes apparent, quietly remove the child to the toileting areas or sick bay and organise clearing up with minimum fuss and talking. There is some evidence that a strong emotional reaction can exacerbate the problem. Reassure the child that this happens for other children from time to time. Once the child is considered capable, involve them in self-care as much as possible. This should not be seen as punitive but a sign of independence and giving them some control. You will need to clarify at a whole school level who is responsible for overseeing this.

Smearing: This is harder for adults to manage but needs a similar approach to soiling. School nurses are well placed to show concern and engage the child in quiet, non-judgmental conversations with open-ended questions such as *'Are you OK – is there anything you want to talk about?'* For those schools who do not have school nurses, teaching assistants may need some training/support if they are required to deal with this.

Engage other children in activities to divert attention.

This behaviour can engender feelings of revulsion that are conveyed to the child who may already be struggling. Staying calm and kind is not always easy.

Longer term change

Establish clear toileting routines to minimize 'accidents'. Not all children will have bodies that evacuate at regular times but it is worth trying. Perhaps the child can choose a soap for their own use.

Teach and encourage self-management as appropriate. You need to know where the child is starting from: awareness of need, level of control, signaling need, motivation etc. The school nurse is an appropriate professional to check this with the child and family.

Have sufficient spare clothing.

Curriculum input on bodily functions, signals, health, hygiene and safety.

Work closely with parents/carers to develop a non-punitive approach.

Provide alternative play materials – such as soft clay perfumed with lavender oil.

Be aware of any potential or actual verbal bullying from peers and take preventative action.

Provide opportunities for talking/listening in a safe space.

Monitor for other behaviours of concern.

The problem: unsafe risk taking

The recipe: taking care of self and others

This behaviour encompasses climbing, throwing objects, dangerous use of school materials and other impulsive behaviours. (See *Impulse control* in **Section 2**.)

What you need to know

Frequency: How often is this happening? Is it increasing or diminishing?

Context: Is there a trigger to unsafe behaviour? In which ways is this behaviour rewarding for the student? Have any responses been effective either at the time or in reducing the behaviour overall?

Strengths: How much is the pupil actually aware of potential danger and in effect protecting themselves and/or others from harm? Is there more control than is immediately apparent?

Other concerns: Is this part of a pattern?

Home: What happens at home?

Today in the classroom

Minimize reactions.

Stay calm and offer the pupil a safe alternative. Use *I statements to focus on desired behaviour, e.g. *'I need you to get down from there'*.

Express care and concern for the pupil.

If the behaviour is accompanied by significant emotion, acknowledge and validate this.

Notice any strengths and show belief in the pupil's ability to re-assert self-control.

Remove audience if possible – especially if they are in potential danger.

If the child does not respond positively, ask a pupil to fetch a second member of staff.

Offer *face-saving solutions.

Ask the student for ideas, e.g. '*I am really worried you will hurt yourself and I am at a loss to know what to do. Can you help me?*'

Longer term change

Help children develop a vocabulary for feelings and encourage them to use this.

Offer regular physical activities that a) produce serotonin that promotes more positive feelings, b) increase the ability to concentrate and c) use up excess energy that is often produced by negative experiences.

Ask the pupil to repeat directions for a class activity – sometimes they have not listened properly and this enhances the chance of alternative negative behaviours.

Model self-talk, e.g. '*That broken window latch banging is driving me nuts. I am going to try and ignore it and ask for it to be fixed by tomorrow*'.

Use a variety of *Circle Solutions activities with the whole class to encourage self-control, dealing with difficult feelings, problem-solving and raising awareness of internal dialogue.

The problem: running away

The recipe: staying safe

What you need to know

Onset: When did this start? Was there a trigger? Is it getting more or less frequent?

Context: What is happening when the pupil stays put? Who is there and what is happening?

Purpose: Is the motivation attention or avoidance? Is the child running away from something or running to somewhere? What emotions are evident?

Response: Is the response used so far exacerbating, maintaining or reducing the problem?

At home: In the child's view, does it make more sense for them to be at home than at school? Issues of family conflict, violence and loss are all relevant here.

Other concerns: Are there related behaviours of concern?

Today in the classroom

Teachers are in a dilemma, because leaving a class to chase a student can be highly rewarding for the pupil seeking attention, but they have a duty of care. There are three options:

- Give a short, clear instruction to do something, e.g. *'Turn around now and walk back to me'*. Give positive feedback for compliance.
- Ask another adult to either gently persuade the pupil back, or follow them to ensure they stay within school grounds. Most school gates are locked after session starts and entry is only gained by permission, but some children may try to climb out. In this case they need to be stopped and others need to be alerted as this puts the pupil in danger.
- Having a 'special place' to run to such as a quiet room may be helpful. It needs to contain nothing much but a couple of cushions or bean bag. This strategy has proved effective in many schools.

*Traffic lights may be helpful and give a child control in another way.

Longer term change

This will depend on the reason for the running and school protocols.

If there is enough space, develop an area in the class for students to go when upset.

Make it difficult to leave. Have the door closed and perhaps put a bell on it so you are alerted if a pupil does try and run.

Discuss with all pupils why staying in class is important.

Establish a positive relationship so the child feels safe and trusts you.

The pupil being able to contact home during the day may also be useful, as may having something from home to carry, such as a piece of cloth sprayed with a familiar scent.

Giving the student choices and leadership opportunities may enhance their sense of responsibility.

Activities need to be sufficiently engaging so the pupil is thinking more of what they are learning than leaving the class.

*Circle Solutions problem-solving activities with the whole class, firstly in pairs or small groups, e.g. 'When someone feels scared what could they do?'

The problem: self-harm

The recipe: positive coping strategies

Primary aged children hurt themselves in many different ways, but only rarely do they intend this to be life-threatening. It is more often an attempt at coping with feelings that are overwhelming. The reaction of the body to physical harm is to produce endorphins which act as pain relief. This can begin a negative cycle, so action needs to be taken promptly to help students learn alternative positive coping strategies. Often the behaviour is secretive as pupils are ashamed and know that the behavior can be alarming to adults when uncovered.

What you need to know

Onset: When did this behaviour start and what was it in response to?

Severity: Is the harm escalating or diminishing?

Perception: What does this pupil say they want to happen?

Today in the classroom

Show concern and empathy. Avoid looking shocked and/or judgmental.

Acknowledge feelings but do not assume what these are; 'upset' is general and useful.

Provide medical aid where needed.

If the pupil is actually self-harming when discovered, then sit close by, put out your hand and gently ask them to give you the instrument they are using. You may want to put your hand on their arm. Take it yourself if the child continues and is in imminent danger. Offer comfort – the student is likely to be distressed.

Inform those in the school responsible for child protection.

Longer term change

Develop a language for emotions and encourage pupils at all times to use words to express feelings.

---

*Circle Solutions activity for sharing coping skills

As with all Circle Solutions activities, this is with all the class not just those at risk:

Mix students up to break up cliques.

Put a number of photos of various scenarios in the middle of the Circle and ask pupils to work in pairs to choose one that might represent a big life challenge. This can include pictures of people getting together, family conflict, exam situations, bullying, losing a match etc. Ask them to think of what feelings might come along with that. Then ask them to think of what someone could do when those feelings become really big and out of control. Share these coping strategies with others in the Circle.

The problem: confusing reality and fantasy

The recipe: awareness of what is real and what is not

This is often a normal developmental stage for pre-school children. Therefore, the older the child the more of a concern this issue might be. Although a rich imagination is to be encouraged, it can be frightening for a child when this gets out of control. The most common outcome is night-time terrors when a child believes the nightmare they have just experienced is real.

When a child has experienced a trauma, fantasy can be a coping mechanism.

Many young children have imaginary friends. This is not a problem because they know that these friends are not real.

What you need to know

Specifics: What is the pupil actually saying? We cannot dismiss issues that may be real, even though they seem unlikely.

Outcomes: What evidence is there that this is impacting on a child's overall well-being? Anxiety, tiredness, relationships, learning?

At home: What do parents/carers say?

Developmental level: Does the pupil behave in ways younger than might be expected for their age in other ways?

Other concerns: Are there other behaviours of concern?

Motivation: Is this a cry for help, a real fear that cannot be otherwise articulated, a need for attention, a way of making sense of something?

Today in the classroom

Keep an open mind and react calmly.

Try not to be judgmental so that the pupil will continue to engage.

Re-focus the pupil into the here and now.

Reassure about what is real.

For older children, you may want to suggest that they write down their 'story'.

Longer term change

Talk to the whole class about the differences between true stories and made-up stories. Give examples. Show how stories can have different endings.

Discuss with families that it might be best to avoid introducing non-real characters at home. The tooth-fairy is fun for most 6–7 year olds, but may be confusing for some.

De-brief children after any role-play or similar activity.

Refer to an outside agency if the fantasy continues and is impacting on everyday functioning.

Resources and further reading

General

Wellbeing Stories: A series of six stories for 9–13 year olds with characters representing positive and negative thinking. The stories deal with test anxiety, transition to high school, loss and depression, organization, perfectionism, entitlement and gratitude. Each comes with a teacher and family toolkit. Each teacher toolkit contains around 20 *Circle Solutions activities. https://www.wellbeingstories.com/

Roffey, S. (2014). *Circle Solutions for Student Wellbeing*. London: Sage Publications.

Avril MacDonald's *Feel Brave Stories* for 4–7 year olds dealing with various issues for young children including loss, exclusion and worries. There is a resource book for teachers: www.feelbrave.com/stories

Restorativeconversation:https://restorativejustice.org.uk/restorative-practice-schools

Cooperative/Collaborative work in the primary school: http://bit.ly/2GmkrS7

Cards and other resources for Circle Solutions activities

Australia: https://innovativeresources.org/product-category/card-sets/

Australia: https://therapeuticresources.com.au/ was originally created for therapists by Quirky Kid but has a much wider use. The Face It cards showing subtle emotions are especially good.

Canada: https://inquiryadventures.com/

UK: https://loggerheadpublishing.co.uk/

UK: https://incentiveplus.co.uk/ This company distributes St Luke's cards such as the symbols cards as well as their own products.

UK: https://atmybest.com/strengths-cards/ These cards have great photos on one side that can be used in many ways.

Getting Things Done

Csikszentmihalyi, M. (1990). *Flow*. New York: Harper and Row.

Dweck, C.S. (2006). *Mindset: The New Psychology of Success*. New York: Random House.

Attention, Focus and Task Completion: https://www.growinggreatschoolsworldwide.com/attention-focus-and-task-completion/

Why Procrastinators Procrastinate: https://waitbutwhy.com/2013/10/why-procrasti-nators-procrastinate.html

Submission by the Food for Life Partnership on Behaviour and Discipline in Schools: https://publications.parliament.uk/pa/cm201011/cmselect/cmeduc/writev/behaviour/we23.htm

https://www.bbcgoodfood.com/howto/guide/behaviour-children-food-and-additives

General Disruption

Sibley, B.A., & Etnier, J.L. (2003). The relationship between physical activity and cognition in children: A meta-analysis. *Paediatric Exercise Science, 15,* 243–256.

To support children with attachment issues:

Bomber, L.M. (2007). *Inside I'm Hurting: Practical Strategies for Supporting Children with Attachment Difficulties in Schools.* Richmond, VA: Worth Publishers.

Geddes, H. (2005). *Attachment in the Classroom: The Links Between Children's Early Experience, Emotional Wellbeing and Performance in School: A Practical Guide for Schools.* Richmond, VA: Worth Publishers.

Social Interactions

Circle of Friends:

http://www.complexneeds.org.uk/modules/Module-3.4-Emotional-well-being-and-mental-health/All/downloads/m12p050c/the_circle_of_friends_approach.pdf

Durlak, J.A., Weissberg, R.P., Dymnicki, A.B., Taylor, R.D., & Schellinger, K.B. (2011). The impact of enhancing students' social and emotional learning: A meta-analysis of school-based universal interventions. *Child Development, 82*(1), 405–432.

The NED approach to bullying: Never Give Up, Encourage others to join you to be Upstanding, Tell someone what is happening: https://www.youtube.com/watch?v=eeqQCyQOCPg

The meanest second grade girl and how others stopped her in her tracks: https://www.youtube.com/watch?v=QFWfFCmjH_s

Emotional Distress

Teaching children about the brain, especially the amygdala: https://www.youtube.com/watch?v=3bKuoH8CkFc

Everyday ideas for teaching young children about emotions: https://www.ecmhc.org/ideas/emotions.html

Separation and divorce: Dowling, E., & Elliott, D. (2012). *Understanding Children's Needs When Parents Separate.* London: Taylor and Francis.

Whitehouse, E., & Pudney, W. (1998). *There's a Volcano in my Tummy: Helping Children to Handle Anger: A Resource Book for Parents, Carers and Teachers.* Gabriola Island, BC: New Society Publishers.

Special Concerns

Autism: National Autistic Society: http://www.autism.org.uk

Foetal Alcohol Syndrome: https://sites.duke.edu/fasd/

Managing Sexualized Behaviour:

   https://www.centralsexualhealth.org/media/6505/msb_guidelines.pdf

   https://www.brook.org.uk/our-work/the-sexual-behaviours-traffic-light-tool

Programs for children to help them keep safe from abuse: www.nspcc.org.uk/preven ting-abuse/keeping-children-safe/underwear-rule/underwear-rule-schools-teaching-resources/

Encopresis:

   https://www.healthychildren.org/English/health-issues/conditions/emotional-problems/Pages/Soiling-Encopresis.aspx

   http://www.handsonscotland.co.uk/topics/toileting/soiling.html

Self-harm: https://www.kidsmatter.edu.au/sites/default/files/public/SelfHarm InformationSheet.pdf

Trauma: https://www.growinggreatschoolsworldwide.com/children-and-trauma/

Index

toileting 34–5, 104, 112, 130–1, 143
traffic lights 20, 35, 45, 49, 100, 103, 111,
    134, 143
trauma 7, 22, 27, 97, 124–5, 126, 130,
    138, 143
trust 4, 14, 84–5, 125, 135
touch 17–18, 56–7, 62, 102, 124

upstanding 82–3, 142

values 7, 13, 85

wellbeing 1, 16, 23, 73, 79, 138, 141–2
whole school 17, 23, 79, 98, 129, 131
words 20, 33, 54, 68–9, 112–13, 137